Twayne's United States Authors Series

Sylvia E. Bowman, *Editor*

INDIANA UNIVERSITY

Nelson Algren

TUSAS 249

Photograph by Stephen Deutch

Nelson Algren

NELSON ALGREN

By MARTHA HEASLEY COX

San Jose State University

and

WAYNE CHATTERTON

Boise State University

TWAYNE PUBLISHERS

A DIVISION OF G. K. HALL & CO., BOSTON

Copyright © 1975 by G. K. Hall & Co.

All Rights Reserved

Library of Congress Cataloging in Publication Data

Cox, Martha Heasley.
  Nelson Algren.

  (Twayne's United States authors series, TUSAS 249)
  Bibliography: p. 149-57.
  1. Algren, Nelson, 1909- — Criticism and inter-
pretation. I. Chatterton, Wayne, joint author.
PS3501.L4625Z66   813'.5'2   74-19223
ISBN 0-8057-0014-5

To Nelson Algren
with Admiration and Affection

Contents

About the Authors

Martha Heasley Cox is Professor of English and Director of the Steinbeck Research Center at San Jose State University, California. With academic degrees from Arkansas College and the University of Arkansas, she has also studied at the universities of Wisconsin and Texas. At present a member of the Executive Committee of the Conference on Composition and Communication and the Board of Directors of the Visual Literacy Conference, she has edited numerous college texts, and one of these, *A Reading Approach to College Writing,* is now in its thirteenth edition. Among her other publications are the *Maxwell Anderson Bibliography,* published by the University of Virginia Press, and articles on Maxwell Anderson and Nelson Algren in the *Encyclopedia of World Literature in the 20th Century.*

Wayne Chatterton is Professor of English at Boise State University and co-editor of the BSU Western Writers Series, which he originated. With academic degrees from Brigham Young University and the University of Utah, he has served as Idaho State Director to the National Council of Teachers of English and as Idaho State Chairman of the NCTE Achievement Awards. He has contributed articles on Hemingway and Faulkner to *College Composition and Communication,* has prepared abstracts on Sinclair Lewis for *Abstracts of English Studies,* and has written *Vardis Fisher: The Frontier and Regional Works,* which is the first of the booklets in the Western Writers Series. In addition to co-authoring the book on Nelson Algren, he has just completed a manuscript on Alexander Woollcott and is preparing one on Irvin S. Cobb, both for Twayne's United States Authors Series.

Preface

Nelson Algren, winner of the first National Book Award for his best-selling novel *The Man with the Golden Arm*, has written three other novels, numerous short stories, travel books, sketches, poetry, essays, prose poems, book reviews, and other literary criticism. His books are all in print, some in several editions. They have been highly successful abroad and, in translation by Jean Paul Sartre and others, are available in several languages. But, despite his stature in contemporary literature, no separately published study — in fact, no serious attempt to comment on or interpret his work at any length — has been made until this one.

Ernest Hemingway once rated Algren second only to William Faulkner as America's greatest novelist. Algren's work does, in some ways, bear comparison to that of Faulkner: Chicago's Division Street becomes as much his territory as Yoknapatawpha County is Faulkner's — so much so that when Studs Terkel's *Division Street, U.S.A.* was published, one reviewer commented that it seemed strange to connect the name of that street with anyone other than Algren. Characters, settings, themes, symbols, imagery, and actual dialogue recur throughout his work as they do with Faulkner. In addition to the derelicts, professional tramps, prostitutes, addicts, convicts, prize-fighters and baseball players, certain characters, with little more than a name change, appear and reappear. The youth, sometimes named Bruno Bicek, who knew he'd "never get to be twenty-one anyhow," is the central character in the frequently anthologized short story "A Bottle of Milk for Mother" and in the second novel *Never Come Morning*. He reappears in both the later novels *The Man with the Golden Arm* and *A Walk on the Wild Side*. The legless man on a platform, whom Algren considers the most significant character he has created, appears in the early short-story collection *The Neon Wilderness* and again as Schmidt in the latest novel *A Walk on the Wild Side*. According to Algren, Schmidt made memorable the musical version of the novel that was presented at the Crystal Palace in Gaslight Square in St. Louis in 1960.

This book is not only an introduction to but an examination of Algren's fiction. Its purpose is to trace his developing talents from his first short story "So Help Me" through his latest published work, *The Last Carousel* (1973). Considerations other than those of chronology, however, have determined the order in which we discuss his work. The first chapter is a literary biography, the longest and most complete of the author yet attempted. Chapter 2 analyzes more than thirty short stories, including several written before and after those collected in *The Neon Wilderness*. Chapter 3 compares and contrasts the first and latest novels, *Somebody in Boots* and *A Walk on the Wild Side*, the latter an "accidental novel," the unexpected result of the author's original intention to prepare the first for republication. A close examination of the two works, comparing theme, characters, style, mood, and plot, offers an unparalleled opportunity to study the changes which occurred in an author and his approach in a time lapse of almost two decades. Chapters 4 and 5 examine the two novels set in Chicago, *Never Come Morning* and *The Man with a Golden Arm*, which are the second and third novels chronologically. The concluding chapter endeavors to assess Algren's importance to and his influence upon contemporary American literature.

No attempt has been made in this book to consider, except incidentally, Algren's poetry, sketches, essays, travel books, book reviews, and other criticism. A study of the poetry in relation to the fiction would be particularly significant in view of the author's recent remarks about the method and chronology of his composition; for, in a letter written in September, 1970, he describes the conception, progression, and completion of image and idea:

I began *Never Come Morning* by doing crayon drawings of a fighter before I knew who he was. Or what I was up to. The drawing became Bruno Bicek. Between *Somebody in Boots* and *Walk* I kept making crayon drawings of a New Orleans whorehouse, seen from the street. That was long before I ever knew that I was going to rewrite the novel into something new. Again, *The Man with the Golden Arm* was a poem before it became a novel. The legless man came in and out of the crayon drawings of the whorehouse, but I didn't write the poems about him until *Walk* was dramatized.

Preface

We are deeply indebted to Mr. Algren not only for his lifetime of work but also, and more personally, for the help he has given and the kindness he has shown during the preparation of this book: the lengthy interviews granted a first time, then graciously repeated when an infallible tape recorder failed; the many letters, phone calls, and return visits; the permission to examine his books, scrap books, manuscripts, and unpublished materials, most of which were unavailable elsewhere; the patience with which he read an early draft of our manuscript and corrected errors in fact, if not judgment. For these kindnesses we dedicate this book to him with our appreciation, admiration, and affection.

MARTHA HEASLEY COX
WAYNE CHATTERTON

Chronology

1909 Nelson Ahlgren Abraham born March 28, in Detroit to second-generation Chicagoans.

1912 Family moved to Seventy-first and South Park, Chicago.

1914- Attended Park Manor Grammar School, Chicago.
1922

1923- Attended Hibbard High School (now Roosevelt High)
1928 in Chicago.

1928- Attended the University of Illinois; graduated with Bachelor
1931 of Science in journalism.

1931- Worked as a door-to-door coffee salesman in New Orleans;
1933 migratory worker in the South and Southwest; co-operator of a gas station near Rio Hondo, Texas; carnival worker. Spent four months in jail at Alpine, Texas, awaiting trial on a charge of stealing a typewriter.

1933 August, published first short story, "So Help Me," in *Story* magazine — a story derived from his gas-station experience.

1935 Published first novel, *Somebody in Boots*, a "Depression" novel. "The Brother's House" included in *O. Henry Memorial Prize Stories*.

1936- Married and divorced. Worked as editor for the Works
1940 Progress Administration Illinois Writers' Project. Served on Venereal Disease Control Program of the Chicago Board of Health. Wrote short stories and poems about dance marathons, whorehouses, and baseball. Father died (1940).

1941 "A Bottle of Milk for Mother" included in *O. Henry Memorial Prize Stories*.

1942 Published *Never Come Morning*, a novel about a Chicago Polish hoodlum-prizefighter involved in rape and murder. "Biceps" included in *Best American Short Stories*.

1942- Served as private in United States Army Field Artillery and

1945 Medical Corps; tours of duty in Wales, Germany, and France. Legally shortened name to Nelson Algren.

1945 Settled down to be "serious about writing" in a room on Wabansia and Bosworth Streets in Chicago. "How the Devil Came Down Division Street" included in *Best American Short Stories.*

1947- Received grants from the American Academy of Arts and
1949 Letters and the Newberry Library as aid in the writing of *The Man with the Golden Arm.*

1949 Published *The Man with the Golden Arm.* Took second trip to Europe (the first, his army experience).

1950 *The Man with the Golden Arm* given the first National Book Award. "The Captain is Impaled" included in *O. Henry Memorial Prize Stories.* Took first trip to Hollywood concerning movie version of *The Man with the Golden Arm.*

1951 Published *Chicago: City on the Make,* an historical and sociological "prose-poem" which "divided Chicago into two almost-armed camps."

1954- Worked on *A Walk on the Wild Side.*
1955

1955- Took second trip to Hollywood (1955). Published *A Walk*
1956 *on the Wild Side* (1956).

1960 Took third trip to Europe — Spain, Greece, Turkey — basis for *Who Lost an American?*

1961 Mother died.

1962 Traveled to Korea, Bombay, Calcutta, and the Philippines — basis for *Notes from a Sea Diary: Hemingway All the Way.*

1963 Published *Who Lost an American?* ("Being a guide to the seamier sides of New York City, Inner London, Paris, Dublin, Barcelona, Seville, Almeria, Istanbul, Crete, and Chicago, Illinois"). Edited a collection of stories titled *Nelson Algren's Own Book of Lonesome Monsters.*

1964 Published, in cooperation with H. E. F. Donohue, a series of interviews titled *Conversations with Nelson Algren.*

1965 Published *Notes from a Sea Diary: Hemingway All the Way* drawn from experiences during his 1962 junket; used personal reflections upon Hemingway as a basis for narration.

1965- Married Betty Ann Jones (1965); divorced (1967). Taught
1967 creative writing at the University of Iowa.

1968- December to May, toured Tokyo, Macao, Saigon, Hong
1969 Kong, Khaosiong, Taipei.

1970 Spent summer (as he had '66 through '69) in Belleville, Illinois, at Cahohen Downs and Fairmont Park. Owned a horse called Jealous Widow. Renamed by associates, "Algren's Folly."

1973 Published *The Last Carousel,* a collection of stories and sketches, some of which appear for the first time in this book; others, usually revised and often retitled for this collection, had appeared previously in periodicals, newspapers, or books.

1974 Taught creative writing at the University of Florida.

The Bard of the Stumblebum

N ELSON Algren's alliance with the world's dispossessed
and downtrodden has encouraged his critics to become
phrasemakers. To Maxwell Geismar, his characters are "the under-
dogs of sin, the small souls of corruption, the fools of poverty."[1]
Malcolm Cowley's phrase "poet of the Chicago slums"[2] seems to
have become a permanent brand, and "Ultima Skid Row"[3] is Leslie
Fiedler's indictment of the narrow world of Nelson Algren. But,
since Algren's world is confined neither to Chicago nor to skid row,
Fiedler is more accurate in characterizing the author as "the bard of
the stumblebum."[4] The stumblebum is Algren's subject — whether
in the North or the South, the city slum, the hobo jungle, the
migratory worker's orchard, or the brothels of Calcutta — wherever
the derelict cries out for recognition and justice.

Since Algren's lifelong residence has been in or near Chicago,
however, and since most of his work has Chicago characters and settings, he has been inescapably associated with Carl Sandburg's "city
of the big shoulders."

I Lineage

Although identified with the Polish-American community, he is
not of that lineage. His paternal grandfather, Nels Ahlgren, was a
Swede whose obsessive but erratic religious convictions drove him
first to Judaism, then to Socialism, and then to Methodism; but at
last he believed that "there is no religion, no truth. It is all
nothing."[5]

According to the novelist's own account, Nels Ahlgren early
became a strict Old Testament fundamentalist, changed his name to
Isaac Ben Abraham, and left Sweden because, "if you became a Jew
in Stockholm at that time, the best thing to do was to go to
America."[6] Reaching America just before the Civil War, the Scan-

dinavian Isaac Ben Abraham joined the Swedish fur traders in Minnesota, where his trading post was burned out in one of the last Indian raids east of the Mississippi.

Moving to Chicago, Ahlgren married a German servant girl. They became squatters at Black Oak, Indiana, where they opened a small grocery and where he made change in Swedish pennies because their value was only one third that of the American penny. When he had used up his Swedish coins, he began minting his own. Headed toward Bethlehem, he next moved to San Francisco, taking his wife but leaving his three children in Indiana. They spent two years in San Francisco trying to get passage money to Jerusalem. The novelist's father was born in this interval.

Isaac Ben Abraham was now a self-appointed rabbi: a religious scold and a tyrannical literal witness to the Old Testament who chastized Jews for their lack of orthodoxy. The San Francisco Jewish community must have felt deeply relieved when Isaac, his wife, and infant son boarded ship in 1870. In the Holy Land, Isaac devoted himself to philosophy and prophecy among other self-appointed prophets. Keeping house for two dozen unemployables exhausted his wife, so she obtained passage money from the American consulate, took her four-year-old son, and left. Isaac joined her aboard ship; and, when he saw the consulate's currency engraved with Washington's head, he quoted the biblical injunction "Thou shalt make no graven image" and threw the money overboard, leaving himself and his wife and son penniless again. Other passengers took up a collection, but Isaac did not get to see the money.

Years later, back in Indiana, he deserted his family for keeps. He became a purchasable missionary, one who adopted any faith for any person or group willing to pay his way anywhere. For sixteen or seventeen years the family heard nothing from, or of, him; then, when he was about sixty years old, he appeared again to spend the winter with them in Chicago. In the spring, his two sons gave the old man a silver dollar and watched him leave on a Madison Street car, and they heard nothing more of him except that he was buried two decades later as a pauper in Florida. Now, declaring a special affinity for this grandfather, Algren asks, "Can pseudo-intellectualism be inherited?"[7]

By 1909, the author's father, age forty-one, was living in Detroit, having married Goldie Kalisher, who had borne him two daughters and who in this year bore the youngest and last child, a boy named Nelson Ahlgren Abraham. She came from a Chicago German-Jewish family which was "always German first"; it spoke German within the household and English in public, but never Yiddish which was "verboten." By the turn of the century, the Kalishers were Americanized.

II *Youth and Education*

After being brought from Detroit to Chicago at the age of three, Nelson attended a Congregationalist Sunday school in a largely Irish neighborhood at Sixty-ninth and South Parkway. As he grew, he came to feel affection for his father; but his feeling was modified by his resentment of the old man's inability to understand movies or to comprehend that policemen took bribes, by his telling the same jokes over and over, and by his incessant references to his job in Detroit at "the screw works."[8] An early sensitivity toward language also provoked Algren's resentment of his mother's misuse of words: "anulimum" for "aluminum" and "pregrant" for "pregnant."

At both Hibbard Junior High School and Roosevelt High School, he was more preoccupied with athletics than with literature. Although far from being a natural athlete, he hung around the gymnasium long enough to become a member of the lightweight basketball squad which won the city championship in 1927:

I was a better clown than an athlete. When I'd drop an easy fly I'd follow through by falling on my face: *anything* for a laugh. I had two nicknames then: my friends called me "Swede" but the basketball coach called me "Clown." After five years of clowning I was graduated 141st in a class of 149. Had the faculty tolerated me for one more semester, I could have passed up those eight idiots behind me. If I couldn't be the brightest kid in sight, I wanted to be the dumbest. Being in between was something unbearable, it seemed.

Algren's sister, Bernice, saw through her younger brother's ploy. Her idea of sending him to a university received sighs from her mother, incredulous muttering from her father, and yelps of gleeful mockery all over the neighborhood. Only bright or rich students went to college in 1927, but Bernice ran the family. She had him enroll at the University of Illinois, loaned him fifty dollars out of her own teacher's salary, and sent him to Urbana. He earned room and board during his four years there by waiting on tables at a graduate fraternity house and by selling sandwiches "at other doors, to fraternity boys cramming into the late hours of the night."

A curious change transpired in his attitude toward books: athletics were nothing; books were all. Though the physical sciences baffled him utterly, humanistic works began to absorb him, particularly those of Matthew Arnold, Thomas Carlyle, Walter Pater, Charles Lamb, Lord Byron, Percy B. Shelley, John Keats, Robert Browning, and Shakespeare:

> For the first time I understood my father was not my father: my grand-father was my father. A sense of identity with him became so strong that it dawned on me: I was him.
> Whether it was the austerity demonstrated by Marcus Aurelius, or preached by Pascal, or something in the genes derived from that mad grand-father, I went, in my second year, into a spiritual phase — using spiritual in the worst sense. All satisfactions of the flesh were banned by my own edict. Any food beyond that sufficient for survival was self-indulgence. To be a man was not to excel physically, not to dominate anyone, but simply to live nobly. In order to live nobly one must think of nothing but poetry and philosophy. The difficulty with sustaining this level of highmindedness — indeed, righteousness — was that when you fell off, you fell awfully far. The more nobly you lived, the deeper the abyss of sin became — and the more appealing. I was certainly a mixed-up kid.

Perhaps while in school and certainly later, Algren was strongly affected by Whitman, whose basic attitudes he has repeatedly reinterpreted. The prefatory quotation for both the short story "A Bottle of Milk for Mother" and his second novel *Never Come Morning* is four lines from Whitman's *Leaves of Grass:*

> I feel I am of them —
> I belong to these convicts and prostitutes myself
> And henceforth I will not deny them —
> For how can I deny myself?

III *Depression Wanderings*

In 1931, Algren was graduated with a Bachelor of Science in journalism and received a credential testifying that its bearer was a qualified editorial-writer. When Algren presented this written evidence to editors from coast to coast, he discovered that no editorial positions were available, not even a newsstand needing a vendor. An editor of the Minneapolis *Journal* did put him to work writing headlines for a week, but on payday he learned there was no paycheck. "I just wanted you to get some experience," the editor explained.

Algren then hitchhiked through the boom towns of East Texas, but he found everybody there so busy getting rich overnight that nobody had time to read a newspaper. He rode freight cars to New Orleans and hit the Old French Market one morning just as the market was opening. He ate a Poorboy sandwich while watching a husky Negro, naked to the waist, decapitating turtles; the headless brutes were stacked in a living pyramid. This scene materialized, a quarter of a century later, in *A Walk on the Wild Side*. Algren recalls another Southern episode, one that occurred when, at twenty-two, he entered a New Orleans store for a Coca Cola: "The sign said Coca Cola was a nickel, and a very attractive girl came out — topless. I just kept looking, like this [standing rigidly erect, eyes fixed forward]. I said, 'Have you got a Coca Cola?' She said, 'Ten Cents' and I said 'I'll drink it here.' And I drank it, my eyes still fixed, and still not knowing where I was." Dove Linkhorn's perception in *A Walk on the Wild Side* is sharper. After spending thirty cents for three nickel cokes and after observing that the girl who makes the sales has one breast tattooed *whiskey* and the other *beer*, he spends a dollar and goes to bed with both.

Another scene from the same book began developing, subconsciously, when Algren sold coffee from door to door for the Standard Coffee Company and used a brightly-colored tin percolator as a gimmick. He also took a door-to-door route for Watkins Products, but that work too did not pay his room rent. His rent was two dollars and thirty-three cents per week, for he shared a seven-dollar-a-week room on Camp Street with two other hustlers, both named Luther.

The Luther from Texas got from a woman's beauty salon a thousand certificates that offered finger waves and shampoos at moderate rates. The trio offered them to housewives with the assurance that the treatments, to women who presented such a certificate, were free. "Just a twenty-five cent courtesy charge," was the pitch; but the twenty-five cent courtesy was payable in advance to the salesman. *A Walk on the Wild Side* contains a long section in which Cass and his buddies, Luke and Fort, as representatives of Madame Dewberry's Beauty Salon, make a good though temporary living selling the same kind of certificates. For Algren and the two Luthers, good times had returned: the hustlers made themselves "ten dollars a day, day in and day out, for two days." On the third day, Luther from Florida was ambushed by two outraged husbands. Algren climbed into a boxcar and slid the doors shut. When he opened them he was in the Rio Grande Valley.

The personal experience gained from this and similar trips lends

verisimilitude to his novels. Whenever his characters are forced by
circumstances to move by freight-car roof, rod, or interior, he sur-
rounds them with catalogues of cabalistic warnings which are saved
from being mere listings by their graphic immediacy: beware Beau-
mont, Greensboro, Boykin; at Waycross you do ninety days in a turp
camp; look out for one-armed Mike Bingo's hole, Flomaton,
Mississippi; look out for Lame Hank Pugh's Marsh City; steer shy of
old Seth Healey, dressed like a Bo but carrying gun and hose-length
in Greenville; but the worst place of all is anywhere in
Georgia. Algren saw the horror of the moving coal and ore car with
its opened dump-bottom; for, if one scrambled into it, one dropped
under the wheels. In two novels, main characters are barely saved
this destiny in a sudden terrible moment: Cass McKay, hero of
Somebody in Boots, is rescued only after a three-mile ride with his
fingers mashed under the boot of his momentary sidekick Thomas
Clay; and in *A Walk on the Wild Side* the neophyte prostitute Kitty
Twist is preserved for the whorehouse only because Dove Linkhorn
is able to seize her overall strap in his teeth until she can scramble to
the edge of the car.

At this time, Algren also began to understand what drives men to
theft. After picking oranges and grapefruit in Southern Texas, he
and the Florida Luther persuaded a local Sinclair Oil agent to let
them open an abandoned filling station near Rio Hondo. Luther, in
a borrowed Studebaker, drove about the Valley buying up black-
eyed peas to be shelled for resale. Algren shelled the peas and
packed them into Mason jars — without making a single sale. Then
he caught Luther stealing the gas, owned by their common enterprise, by syphoning it into the Studebaker. Algren sanded the
remaining gas and moved on, and this experience was the basis for
his first short story, "So Help Me."

Meanwhile, Algren kept moving from town to town. Sometimes
he was held overnight on a vagrancy charge, then released in the
morning with the understanding that he was to keep moving on. At
LaFeria, Texas, he was taken on as a shill by a team operating a
phony chance-wheel at a county fair. One of the wheel's owners, a
tall man wearing a Texas rancher's hat and boots, stood in the
midway watching for the sheriff as well as for a victim. When he
spotted a "mark," he signalled his partner, and the partner spun the
wheel. The three shills — with Algren in the middle — set up a
gleeful clamor as they began winning silver dollars with every turn

of the wheel. The game was to get a mark in front of the wheel and bet on it. Algren tells what happened:

> I won a bunch of money, but with a pair of old-time carnies leaning on me from both sides, there wasn't any way of getting any of it into my pockets. My pay was sufficient to buy a couple hamburgers and a cup of coffee twice a night, but I wanted a raise. So I waited until I saw the sheriff making his rounds of the midway, and darted to his side with six silver dollars in my pocket. The sheriff studied his new companion, but all I wanted was to walk beside him. Near the carnival gate I lost myself in the crowd — but didn't take the chance of leaving by the gate itself. I felt that one of the carnies — or both — might be wanting to see me about something. So I got through a fence in the darkness and stumbled about till I reached the Santa Fe tracks. The carnies would have had to be on horseback to catch me after that.

"I'm still running," he observes self-mockingly, then continues the tale of his meandering:

> After finding other holes in the darkness of other fences, I headed for El Paso atop a box-car. From the roof of the car I could see the engine, a half a mile ahead, winding slowly through the mountains. And as I came through a pass I saw a lovely, homesick sight: the white and shining halls and spires of a campus. It was Sul Ross College. For the first time, then, it came to me that I wasn't what I thought I was. I wasn't an editorial writer. I wasn't a columnist. I wasn't even a police reporter or a desk man writing obituaries: I was a bum. I decided to go back to college.
>
> I climbed down off the cars, made a room-with-board arrangement at a dilapidated ranch-house on the outskirts of town and began attending Sul Ross without bothering to register. I simply walked into a room occupied by nothing but covered typewriters, took the cover off one and began typing. What I was typing didn't matter: it was plain that a man operating a typewriter in a college classroom wasn't a bum.
>
> The idea worked, but I overworked it. With a half-finished story in one of the machines, I decided to finish it in Chicago. But on *what?* I didn't have a typewriter in Chicago. So I simply picked up the machine, the story still in it, and walked down the main street of Alpine, Texas, with the typewriter in my arms. I stopped at a market to pick up a wooden box big enough to hold the machine, packed it in my room — the story still in it — and took it down to the freight depot for shipping to Chicago. That done, I caught the next train east, confident that the machine would catch up with me in Chicago.
>
> The machine never left Alpine. I got as far as Sanderson, Texas. I was sunning myself a few yards from the tracks, waiting for my train to get moving again, when a man with a badge stepped up and asked me my name. I told

him and the man advised me that he had to take me back to Alpine. Something about a typewriter. Betrayed by a freight-master!

IV *Prisoner of the State*

The ensuing four or five months provided Algren with the raw, firsthand material which was to inform some of the best jailhouse episodes in his fiction. He readily admits the closeness of his fiction to actual experience, but he insists upon basic qualifications: "I always draw autobiographically — I mean emotionally, you know. Emotionally it's all autobiographical. But chronologically it's not at all."

Awaiting the periodic arrival of a circuit-riding judge, he was jailed from November to March. In that jail he lived the painful, often brutal scenes which, heightened and dramatized, recur like jailbird nightmares wherever his fiction depicts the small, tight world of the imprisoned. There, perhaps for the first time, he experienced the inverted social and legal values by which society judges the underdog as a creature who is different, in kind as well as degree, from those higher in the "pecking order."

The setting became almost a stereotype in Algren's portrayal of Southern jails: one good-sized cell-block with perhaps four individual cells, each large enough for three or four men. These cells were used mostly for sleeping and for storage of meager private effects like eating utensils. Here Algren became acquainted with a representative cross-section of jailbirds, whose characteristics he later fictionized. Among those with whom Algren shared the cell-block were a one-armed man who bent tobacco tins with his calloused nub; an eccentric rodeo rider charged with two murders, who devised a jailhouse game in which the participants whacked each other with a belt; a likable Mexican; and a prisoner brought there to die after being shot trying to escape. At one point during his term, Algren was afflicted with a case of "traveling hives" which broke out wherever he scratched himself. He refused the sheriff's offer of an insecticide, knowing such a cure would be worse than the disease. These elements became fused in the "tank scenes" of *Somebody in Boots* and "El Presidente de Méjico."

The man with a nub for an arm becomes Nubby O'Neill of *Somebody in Boots;* and, with his arm restored, he is the murderer, Jesse Gleason, of "El Presidente de Méjico." Both characters are persecutors of any Mexican inmates of the jail. The original Mexican of the El Paso County jail, whose unborn son Algren jokingly predicted would become the President of Mexico, was the model for Salomon Rivera in *Somebody in Boots* and for Portillo in the short story. Rivera was brutally beaten with a belt, but Portillo was shot and killed, as was the real-life prisoner. For novelistic purposes, Algren magnanimously lends his own traveling hives to Nubby's imbecilic lackey, Creepy, who likewise declines the insecticide treatment.

When Algren came to trial, the jury found him guilty but recommended mercy. The judge, who sentenced him to two years at Huntsville, suspended the sentence when Algren promised to leave the state and return to Chicago. Since the gas station experience, he had become more and more disillusioned with the "condition of the Confederacy"[9] — a reaction which he conveyed by letter to his friend Murray Gitlin in Chicago.

V   *A Career is Launched*

Reaching the familiar scenes of his home city, Algren found Gitlin serving as the director of the Jewish People's Institute on Douglas Boulevard and conducting a writers' workshop. Algren joined the group. When Gitlin insisted that the gas station account contained the elements of a story, Algren elaborated it. Gitlin sent it to *Story* magazine, which launched Algren's career by publishing it under the title "So Help Me." When a following form letter inquired whether the author of "So Help Me" was working on a novel, Algren responded by hitchhiking to New York and presenting himself to James Henle of Vanguard Press. Henle advanced him ten dollars against a contract calling for ninety dollars more, and this sum was to be paid to Algren at thirty dollars a month for three months.

VI   *The First Novels*

Algren admits that he was not sure what a novel was, that he thought a writer worked up his material from other books. Nevertheless, he created a remarkable first novel, a story of aimless wandering drawn almost entirely from his own experience. Three-quarters through the book Cass McKay, the illiterate final descendant of the "hunters of Kentucky," had ridden box-cars east and west, north and south so many times, he said, that now his travels were "mixed up in his head" and he "no longer remembered just where he *had* been." Algren's purpose seems to have been to dramatize the sheer purposelessness of such wanderings, ones based largely upon Algren's own meanderings.

On the market, the novel was not a success, but reviewers took it seriously.[10] This first novel is important also because Algren packs into a single panoramic entity the situations and locales which, separately, form the bases for his future novels: the South with its peculiar world of drunks, pimps, whores, freaks, hicks, monsters, and perverts; Chicago with — besides the drunks, pimps, whores, and freaks — its urban concentration of card sharps, prizefighters, coneroos, smalltime hoodlums, and dope-heads.

In the summer of 1936, Algren was married and looking for work, which he found as an editor on the Illinois Writers' Project at eighty-seven dollars a month; but this stipend was to be graduated over the next four years to a hundred and twenty-five. During this interval, Algren was more preoccupied with poetry than with the novel, publishing his poems in *Poetry, Southern Review,* and *Esquire.* Algren avoids discussing his first marriage, saying "Marriage was simply distracting, that was all." After a divorce in 1940, he secluded himself on Chicago's Northwest side to write his first Chicago novel, *Never Come Morning,* which was published in 1942.

Drawn from the lives of people Algren had known, this story traces inexorably, but with compassion, the steady movement of Bruno Bicek toward defeat in his struggle against the social and statutory laws which govern his world. A Polish "punk" aspiring to the hierarchy of hoodlumism, torn between prizefighting and pitching baseball as his means of ascent, and so bound by the arcane demands of his neighborhood tribe that he "sets" a term in jail for another's crime and sacrifices his girl friend Steffi to an unforgettable gang rape, he chooses to emerge as the pugilistic "white hope" Bruno "Lefty" Biceps. He wins the big prizefight, only to lose all else in the larger struggle against larger forces that are represented by the weary, seasoned police Captain, One-Eye Tenczara, who, like a doomsday figure, clamps upon Bruno the guilt for the alley-fight murder of a Greek interloper into the long-past gang rape of Steffi.

Algren's second novel was better integrated than the first, for he achieved in it, unity "of action, mood, and form."[11] Though one reviewer felt that Algren was too preoccupied with gang life for its own sake,[12] another recognized the thematic strength of a powerful story devoted to portraying the lives of poor people who can live only by victimizing others who are even poorer.[13] Indeed, this novel presented the theme so strongly that the Polish Roman Catholic Union succeeded in having it banned from the Chicago Public Library.

Most reviewers heralded the new novel as a significant addition to the long-recognized school of "Chicago novelists" — including Theodore Dreiser's *Sister Carrie* and Upton Sinclair's *The Jungle*, the work of James T. Farrell and Richard Wright, all of whom perpetuate a strong tradition of social protest. Though not primarily a novelist, Carl Sandburg somehow epitomized the Chicago group's tradition. Looking back in 1969, Algren said that nobody writing seriously of the 1930-1950 Chicago scene could have failed to be influenced by the tradition: "It was in the air." He adds, however, that "other than Sandburg, I never felt any impact from Anderson, Farrell, Dreiser or any of the others."

VII *Private Algren*

Among other things "in the air" during the late 1930's and early 1940's, however, was impending war. Algren felt deeply·about the ideological principles which were at stake in the Spanish Civil War. Though never a member of the Communist party, he sympathized with the Loyalists in Spain, and he had worked with people whom he knew to be Communists. But, by the time he began work on *Never Come Morning*, he had "simply moved away from them" because he could not abide their authoritarianism.

From 1942 to 1945, Algren served in the United States Army Field Artillery and Medical Corps. As far as his writing is concerned, Algren's army experiences were largely unfruitful. With perverse pride, he is fond of saying that he entered the army as a private, was discharged as a private, and was never awarded a good-conduct ribbon. Between induction and discharge, he spent a year with the field artillery at Fort Bragg and at Camp Maxey, Texas; about three months at Camp Penally, Wales; a short period of time in Germany with the Medical Corps during the Battle of the Bulge; and a concluding stint in Marseille, a "Wild West" town then, where he quickly became conversant with the waterfront neighborhoods and the machinations of the black market.

The only writings which can be directly linked with these experiences are five short stories, "He Couldn't Boogie-Woogie Worth a Damn," "That's the Way It's Always Been," "Pero Venceremos," "No Man's Laughter," and "The Heroes," and some incidental perspective-references in the 1960 "travel-book" *Who Lost an American?* Though Algren felt that material for a "big book" was implicit in the "Boogie-Woogie" story — an American soldier has deserted and is living off the black market with a French girl — he could not generate enough interest to develop that potential; instead, he assembled the collection *The Neon Wilderness* in Chicago.

VIII   *Writing in Earnest:* The Neon Wilderness

In 1945, at the age of thirty-six, Algren deliberately sought haven from wandering. The aimless bindlestiff existence of the Depression years, the unsatisfactory pursuit of political and ideological causes, the forced vagabondage of military life — all these had instilled in him a yearning to settle in some familiar place where he could do serious, sustained writing. He chose on Wabansia and Bosworth Streets in Chicago an austere but clean two-room flat with a bedroom and toilet but no bath or shower. To bathe, he went to the Young Men's Christian Association, where he also kept trim and alert, as he has throughout his life, by swimming and bag-punching.

He spent 1945 and 1946 collecting, writing, and rewriting the twenty-four short stories of *The Neon Wilderness*, seven of which had been published previously. Often loosely constructed, sometimes hardly more than slice-of-life studies, frequently nightmarish and grotesque, but always vital, concrete, and carefully selective in detail, these twenty-four stories are a compendium of the settings and motifs which are characteristic of Algren's fiction. Generally defined, the stories cover a broad spectrum: police interrogation is the subject of two stories; prostitution, three; gambling, six; army life, five; incarceration and release, three; and prizefighting, two. The collection also contains a neighborhood ghost story; a saloon story; and the titular jungle-motif story, "Design for Departure." Five of the stories have appeared either in O. Henry Memorial collections or in *Best American Short Stories;* and two, "How the Devil Came Down Division Street" and "A Bottle of Milk for Mother," have been widely anthologized.

IX   *Recognition: Grants and Awards*

In 1947, the American Academy of Arts and Letters awarded Algren a thousand dollars in recognition of the novel *Never Come Morning* which, in the judges' opinion, had not received the notice it deserved. At about the same time, Algren received a grant of a thousand dollars from the Newberry Library to further the writing of *The Man with the Golden Arm*. In 1947, Algren also met Simone de Beauvoir, who recounts in her autobiography her meeting Algren in Chicago, their 1948 trip down the Mississippi and to Mexico, his visit to Paris and their conversations with Sartre, and her return in both 1950 and 1951 to visit Algren in Miller, Indiana. In *America Day by Day*, she included a lengthy description of their relationship; in *The Mandarins*, a work dedicated to Algren, she fictionalized the affair. By the time her autobiography was published, Algren wished to forget the widely publicized love affair. "She's fantasizing a relationship in the manner of a middle-aged spinster,"[14] he said. "*Will she ever quit talking?*"[15]

Algren's next novel, *The Man with the Golden Arm*, received the first National Book Award in 1950. Using a title drawn from a Chicago dice-player's habitual remark that he had a golden arm, Algren relates the nightmare existence of thirty-year-old army veteran Frankie Majcinek, who is known as "The Dealer" Frankie Machine for the mechanical precision with which his golden arm manages the dice game at Schwiefka's gambling parlor. With always a glimmer of hope, but foredoomed to perish in the streets, alleys, and tenement corridors of Division Street, Frankie Machine struggles with the irreversible insanity of a wife crippled by his own drunken automobile accident; with the futile ministrations of a too-casual mistress; with a minion who fails him under expert pressures applied by the veteran police captain "Record-Head" Bednar; and at last with the "thirty-five pound monkey on his back," which drives him to murder his dope supplier and to foil earthly justice by hanging himself with a length of twine taken from a bundle of old newspapers.

The penetrating gaze which Algren fastens upon the lives of Division Street derelicts, the alternation of lyricism and hardcast prose which had also characterized *Never Come Morning*, and the sense of authority in details of scene and nuances of speech offended some readers and reviewers; but, by general consent, the story achieved strong thematic force and presented memorable characters.

Charges that Algren had approached too near sentimentality in his love for the unlovable — for what Leslie Fiedler later called "The Noble Savages of Skid Row"[16] — and that the last portion of the tale was a cop-and-robber cliché have persisted, but not entirely without justice, as the author himself has realized. Asked in 1959 what he would change in the book, he said that he would avoid the "cowboy and Indian ending."[17] Nevertheless, most critics and reviewers first seriously considered Algren on the appearance of *The Man with the Golden Arm*.

X Misadventures in Hollywood

Hollywood was also interested. In 1955, Algren, carrying a movie script done with a collaborator, met Otto Preminger in Hollywood. The producer spoke with him only twice — just long enough to say that the *Golden Arm* script was not acceptable and to ask for another treatment. Algren, incensed by Preminger's attitude, dashed off a deliberately frivolous twelve-page treatment to demonstrate his contempt; and Preminger got the point.

The story had been sold by Roberts Productions to Preminger and Carlyle Productions for an undisclosed sum, but Algren received an original sale fee of only $15,000. Later, Algren filed suit, charging illegal use of credit-lines and failure to yield profits due to him from the film version. Both the Film Writers' Guild and The Authors' League of America supported his suit; and Rex Stout, vice-president of the Authors' League, said in 1956 that "To have that novel turned into a motion picture advertised as 'A Film by Otto Preminger,' is certainly not a pleasant experience and for most writers would be intolerable."[18] Algren eventually dropped the suit because of lack of funds.

The movie broke the taboo against drug addiction as a film theme, but it received little acclaim. Algren now recalls that Robert Hatch wrote in *The Nation:* "The book had respect for its people; the film is contemptuous of them." "This," Algren adds, "is because I wrote the book and Preminger made the movie."[19] Algren has written two pieces on his Hollywood experiences: one, which appeared in *The Nation*, is called "Hollywood Djinn";[20] the other, included in *The Last Carousel* (1974), is "Otto Preminger's Strange Suspenjers."

XI Chicago: City on the Make

Back in Chicago after his Hollywood misadventure, Algren composed one of the most remarkable documents of his career — a prose-poem which bared and charted the subconscious motives of the lakeside city as though a poetic psychiatrist had published notes preserved from lake-bed sessions with it. The Freudian cast of this analogy is supported by Algren's own imagery which renders *Chicago: City on the Make* (1951) a Chicagoan's lovesong to a fickle but fascinating mistress.

In favorably comparing Algren's prose-poetry with Sandburg's "Chicago poems," Budd Schulberg rightly noticed that Algren had founded his song upon the tension between language and substance which is characteristic of good poetry. To Schulberg, the tension of

Chicago: City on the Make resides largely in the montage-like superimposition of the "New Chicago" upon the old, a tension which "Algren passes on to us from . . . the city he loves like a beat-up old harridan whose youthful charms only he remembers."[21] The tension lies also in the tightness with which Algren fuses "metaphorical fireworks"[22] and poetic syntax into prose paragraphs whose substance is often the mundane, harsh, or even cynical socio-historiography of his material. The effect is unlike that of any other work in American letters.

In an introduction appended to the "Contact Edition" ten years later, Algren justifies the material and its treatment as a demonstration of his view that "literature is made upon any occasion that a challenge is put to the legal apparatus by a conscience in touch with humanity." The definition is, of course, applicable to all of his fiction and, as he prefers to believe, to literature in general. But applied specifically to the city "on the make," the definition supports his main thesis that Chicago began, grew, developed, and yet remains Hustler Center, U.S.A.: a city "that was to forge out of steel and blood-red neon, its own peculiar wilderness."

This urban wilderness is a forced mutation of the original wilderness of lakeside forest and plain, territory conned from the Indians by "Dauntless Pioneers," a euphemism for people who "were out to make a fast buck." And the new wilderness has been a hustler's city ever since — a ball game rigged against the undying efforts of the Do-Gooders. "An infidel's capital," it was the stomping ground of Reed Waddell, originator of the gold-brick bunko; of Mickey Finn, knockout-drop pioneer; of Hinky Dink Kenna, the hustler's hustler. But it was also the city of Jane Addams of Hull House; of baseball's Shoeless Joe Jackson; of the white-haired poet Carl Sandburg. It is a two-faced city: "One for poets and one for promoters. One for the good boy and one for the bad." In this metropolitan Janus, "always our villains have hearts of gold and all our heroes are slightly tainted."

In an introduction and an epilogue written for the first and third printings of the 1961 edition, Algren re-examines the decade-old prose poem; and he discovers that the most significant change in the metropolis since the essay first appeared is not finer buildings or efficient expressways but "a change of heart." It has turned cold, and the hope of the past is gone.

The book has never been popular in Chicago. The Chicago *Daily News* editorialized, upon its appearance, that the book was "A Case for Ra(n)t Control." The *Tribune* felt that its appeal was limited to masochists. It has, nonetheless, had some impact in New York City and around San Francisco. Two editions have been brought out in the Bay Area. Sections of it were translated, by Jean-Paul Sartre, for *Temps Modernes*, and an Italian translation has been made.

The recently added epilogue of almost a thousand lines is a clever, hard-hitting pastiche, partly a recurring parody of a medley of Sandburg,

> Hog-Butcher, Stacker-of-Wheat, Freight-Handler . . .
> All-Around-Rotating-Fink-To-The-Nation,

partly capitalized newspaper lines after the manner of Dos Passos, partly sequential mock-quotations from newspaper columnists, partly prose anecdotes, but mostly lyrics which are highly typical Algren. Pursuing the theme that

> Only in a city whose pleasures are pure
> Does sin anger the rich
> If the sinner is poor

Algren resorts to prose to answer the periodic claims that Chicago is in the grip of a renaissance. "A renaissance," he argues, "does not happen to concrete and steel. . . . A renaissance happens to people."

XII *An Accidental Novel*

Algren's next major work, and to date his last, *A Walk on the Wild Side* (1956) is, in his terms, "an accidental novel." In 1954, Algren accepted an advance of fifteen hundred dollars for a paperback reprint of *Somebody in Boots*. The publisher wished to capitalize on the popularity of *The Man with the Golden Arm* by reissuing the early novel. But when Algren reread the book, he discovered it to be so rhetorical that he felt he had to revise it. Neither he nor his editor foresaw that, in the rewriting, a new novel would develop.

Algren had originally titled his first novel *Native Son*, borrowing a current political term which was used in 1932 to designate a dark-horse presidential candidate from California. When publishers demurred that the title was misleading since the book had nothing to do with either California or any political son, the title became *Somebody in Boots*, one which, though it seemed meaningless to

Algren, was lifted out of the context of the manuscript. Later, when talking with his friend Richard Wright, Algren mentioned the loss of the preferred title, and Wright asked permission to use it.

After substituting *A Walk on the Wild Side* for the original title, Algren, continuing his preparations for the reissue, became dismayed at his early mannerisms:

It was deadly. It was such schoolboy poetry, you know, very consciously poetic, and inverted sentences, and I thought, "Oh, boy!" So I corrected the first page — you know, I crossed out this and then I crossed out that, and then I started pasting in. I didn't know I was writing a new book. And then it began to strike me as very funny: in every chapter some child had her head cut off, and you know I was really laying it on, and twenty years later it was silly, and so — pompous. So I kept making it funny. And this guy that was so grim in there at the beginning just became a stud, a big, silly stud.

Algren then reworked the entire twenty-year-old story, but he fulfilled his original intent of exploring the destiny of a truly dispossessed native son, a modern descendant of "that gander-necked clan" of frontier stock which the advance of civilization had "left landless as ever in sandland." Thus out of Cass McKay was born Dove Linkhorn of Arroyo.

Algren decided to write "a good, cheap, corny" reader's book, instead of a writer's book. The accident of its genesis did not prevent the author from seeing that the formlessness of the earlier book had to be overcome. Yet too much preparation and deliberation, he had learned, can be a handicap: "If you resolve to write this great short story or this great book and you plod day after day, and you . . . pile everything into it, you come up with a great stone brick of some kind. There's no spontaneity in it. But sometimes if you're very lucky . . . you're preoccupied with something, and then things come in that you would have excluded."

A Walk on the Wild Side, then, is just such a happening: the metamorphosis of Cass McKay into Dove Linkhorn, son of the "lonesome wife-left feller" Fitz Linkhorn, whose public denunciations of the Roman Catholic Church are derived from a bottle. Like Cass, Dove has a brother; but he is no longer the grim and brutal Bryan of *Somebody in Boots;* he is the hounded Byron who, astride a cannon, is dying of a cough while defying his father's prophetic howlings.

Dove goes to New Orleans and fulfills his destiny by becoming a peep-show performer — a natural stud whose back-country shrewdness and undrainable sexual powers make him a peerless pimp and a peep-show lecher.

Most of the influential reviewers were shocked by the new Algren offering. They challenged Algren's stance as a champion of the dispossessed while he denigrated the possessors. Leslie Fiedler accused him of striking a pose more obvious than Hemingway's, of using an artificial style to pack the story with encyclopedic lists of local-color detail, and of editorializing.[23] Norman Podhoretz, who could not agree that outcasts are better than respectable people, charged Algren with creating an incompatible alternation of the sordid and the poetic, "as though Pollyanna were writing 'The Grapes of Wrath' in dactylic hexameters."[24] *Time* followed suit,[25] but others regarded the book as an important contribution to modern American literature. James T. Farrell, conceding that Algren wrote only of society's lost souls, praised the novel as "the product of a distinguished American writer."[26] After more than a decade, Algren himself considers *A Walk on the Wild Side* by far his best novel, "an American fantasy written to an American beat as true as *Huckleberry Finn*."[27] And today of all the major works of Algren, this novel has the greatest vitality.

XIII   *Travel and Travel Books*

Algren went to Europe in 1960 and to Southeast Asia in 1962, 1968, and 1969. From his experiences during the 1960 trip, he drew the material for his first travel book, *Who Lost an American?* The book is dedicated to his early travel companion, Simone de Beauvoir, and includes his report of their 1949 sojourn in Paris. It also takes the reader on a tour of London, Paris, Dublin, Barcelona, Seville, Almeria, Istanbul, Crete — and New York and Chicago.

Actually, the "tour," organized under geographic section headings, is less literally a trip than Algren's own special brand of Impressionistic reactions to people, things, ideas, places — all lodged somewhere in a creative imagination from which he shapes his often sharp, often bizarre, sometimes tender, but always entertaining episodes and characters, whether real or imaginary — which inhabit this tourist's world. Relying upon his own impressions, Algren moves as he wishes through time and place as he commiserates with South European beggars; slashes at Norman Mailer, whom he dubs Manlifellow; side-swipes exhibitionist artists and writers; and analyzes the true lostness of the Coca Cola American in the mysterious East. But he is most truly lost among the cunning "what-makes-Sammy-run" publishers, writers, and entrepreneurs of New York. And he is most disturbed to find himself lost in the city which had always seemed his own — to return to an installment-plan, high-rise, freeway-veined, Playboy-Club Chicago to which he is a stranger.

Generally, reviewers were not sure what attitude to assume toward a book whose genre was so unfamiliar. Many were disappointed that Algren had chosen to spend his time and talents on such work. Predictably by now, others were offended at his indulgence in personal prejudices and at his penchant for taking potshots at people he disliked. A few, like Herbert Gold, found this particular narrative medium an effective vehicle for a quality they had learned to respect, "Algren's personal rhythm — irreverent, funny, surreal, as if he has blended the lyricism of his early writing . . . with a tough meander and wail."[28] The mere titles of substantial reviews indicate the tone which characterized the critics' attitudes. Besides Norman Mailer's self-defensive and condescending *Esquire* review titled "The Big Bite,"[29] there were William Barrett's "Citizens of the World,"[30] Hilton Kramer's "He Never Left Home,"[31] *The Times Literary Supplement's* "Un-American Notes,"[32] *Newsweek's* "Baedeker with a Bite,"[33] and *Time's* "Intellectual as Ape Man."[34]

Another addition to the travel-book genre was *Notes from a Sea-Diary: Hemingway All the Way* (1965). This new "Baedeker" tells of Algren's 1962 voyage as the *Malaysia Mail's* lone paid passenger from Seattle to Korea, Bombay, Calcutta, and China Sea ports. Incensed at Hemingway's detractors, some of whom were also his own, and armed with essays written by the most vitriolic of these critics, Algren boarded ship determined to pay a long overdue debt by writing the first seafaring essay upon the man — and his critics. Algren's account of his meeting with Hemingway in Cuba in 1955 is more highly Impressionistic than anything in *Who Lost an American?* To critics like Morley Callaghan, who failed to recognize Algren's purpose, his Surrealistic approach seemed a clownish and superficial attempt, one more revelatory of Algren than of Hemingway.[35]

In the early notes from Algren's personal log, he roves among the members of the crew, meeting in turn the indefinable purser Manning; the boil- and clap-ridden lecher and card-sharp Crooked-Neck Smith; the ship's carpenter and Southeast Asian veteran Chips; and the radio operator, the inevitable "Sparks," surname of Concannon. These are portraits of men after the familiar manner of Algren's

Division Street and French Quarter types, just as the many women he meets in ports are exotic sisters of the universal Woman of Chicago and New Orleans. One section of the travelogue is, in fact, a series of fallen-female case studies like those included in *Never Come Morning.*

With some justice, most of the reviewers concurred that in this narrative Algren had gone too far out of his way to obliterate his enemies as well as Hemingway's. His insistent war against Fiedler, Podhoretz, Dwight Macdonald, Leon Edel, and Burton Rascoe left him open to the charge that he had produced a "diatribe within a narrative"[36] in the form of the modern confessional.[37]

Once again some critics marveled at Algren's ability to concoct structural and stylistic mixtures unlike any others,[38] but another condemned his abrupt shufflings of hard-muscled prose and lyric poetry.[39] To one, he had become "just good old bleary, balding, middle-aged Nelson, the Edgar Guest of the seamy side."[40] But to a critic more sympathetically tuned to Algren's talents and sensibilities, his "passionate, honest, and moving defense becomes a hymn to Hemingway from the lower depths."[41]

Seeing the world from the point of view of those about whom he has written, Algren has lived among dope addicts without becoming addicted, among alcoholics without becoming an alcoholic, and among criminals without turning to crime; but he reminisces about moments when he recognized that the dangers were real. The episode, recorded in the *Sea Diary*, of the attack by a crazed, knife-wielding sailor is drawn, impressionistically, from life. Algren remembers that he was scrambling down a hallway, not running but leaping like an impala, and that he realized he had no right to be there: "I was thinking, 'This could never happen to Saul Bellow.' You know, it wasn't a criticism of Bellow. It was a criticism of myself. . . . At three o'clock in the morning, I ought to be asleep in my little nest in Chicago and instead I'm running, scared to death, down the top floor of a tenement in Calcutta with an insane sailor with a bread-knife chasing me. Something is wrong. Something is really wrong."

XIV *Compilations, Conversations, and Lectures*

Sandwiched between the two travel books were two other strange mixtures: one, a collection of short stories titled *Nelson Algren's Own Book of Lonesome Monsters*, a compilation "arranged" by his agent in order to pay him a $1000 advance for his 1962 boat trip; the other, a product of H. E. F. Donohue's thirteen tape-recorded sessions which appeared as *Conversations with Nelson Algren* in 1964. Though Algren's agent selected most of the stories for *Lonesome Monsters*, she and Algren agreed that the stories would represent the power and prevalence of a contemporary theme suggested by a passage in *A Walk on the Wild Side:* "the city was full of lonesome monsters."

The selections, modern nightmare studies, written by Joseph Heller, Donohue, Bruce Jay Friedman, Terry Southern, James Blake, Saul Bellow, James Leo Herlihy, Thomas Pynchon, and others, support Goethe's famous statement "I have never heard of a crime of which I am not myself capable," which Algren uses as epigraph. The last story of the collection is Algren's adaptation of the "Mammy Freak" episode from *A Walk on the Wild Side*. In this version he re-instates a character deleted from the novel at the editor's request. This character, based on a defrocked priest whom Algren had known in Paris, "believed that he could prove by parthenogenesis that Jesus was a dwarf."

Most reviewers considered Algren's short introduction to the collection to be fully as important as the stories it introduced. One objected to his conclusions largely on the premise that an artist who evokes a monster must at least control him; that, unlike Algren, most of the authors were at least personally disengaged from their monsters; and that a monster's monstrous crimes cannot be condoned merely because the crimes are human and therefore deserving of understanding by other lonesome monsters.[42]

The *Conversations* are the most comprehensive of the growing list of Algren interviews, including those by Alston Anderson and Terry Southern, David Ray, J. W. Corrington, and the most recent unpublished ones by the authors of this study. Deliberately unstructured and wide-roving, the *Conversations* between a young writer and the established author were by turns static and supercharged, sometimes striking spontaneous sparks, occasionally bogging down or doubling back. Though most reviewers found the repartee fascinating, many thought Algren too voluble, rambling, or self-dramatizing.[43] And despite the fact that reviewers found Donohue effective, even refreshing, he sometimes seemed determined to get Algren to say what he wished to hear.

In 1965, Algren married Betty Ann Jones. Though the marriage ended in divorce in 1967, Algren makes a point of saying that they are still good friends. He spent the school year 1965-1966 as lecturer in creative writing at the University of Iowa, where he found both the teaching experience and the association with a colleague, Kurt Vonnegut, Jr., rewarding. He became convinced during that year, however, that one cannot "teach creative writing any more than he can teach conformism or teach people how to react. If he's a creative writer, he wouldn't be there, because creativity is a lone enterprise."

In 1968, Algren wrote the Introduction for *The True Story of Bonnie and Clyde as told by Bonnie's Mother and Clyde's Sister.* Algren's more succinct title for his contribution was "How Do I Look Boys Dead or Alive?" Placing Bonnie and Clyde in historical perspective and in the climate of their times, Algren reveals them as "outcasts of the cotton frontier" and as "children of the wilderness whose wilderness had been razed." Rejecting the life of a cotton chopper or sharecropper, they chose instead to run like "two terrified foxes" for their lives; and, in the process, they created a myth, an aura of the supernatural, which survived their deaths.

Since his boat trip to Saigon in 1968-1969, Algren has produced a steady stream of articles, essays, sketches, book reviews, and short stories. Sometimes he participates in panel discussions and colloquia which are produced by television stations in the Chicago area. In his lectures to college groups and other gatherings throughout the nation, he frequently concludes his remarks with the words of Cross Country Kline, a character in *A Walk on the Wild Side.* From Algren's years of wandering, his intense observation of human behavior, and his attempts to write honestly about the world he knows, he has learned that Kline's advice is the best anybody can offer those who wish to survive:

Never play cards with a man called Doc.
Never eat at a place called Mom's.
Never sleep with a woman whose troubles are worse than your own.
. . . life is hard by the yard, son.
But you don't have to do it by the yard.
By the inch it's a cinch.

CHAPTER 2

The Contour of Human Life

CRITICS such as Chester Eisinger, George Bluestone, Maxwell Geismar, and Leslie Fiedler, who have assessed Algren's fiction comprehensively, have approached the major works chronologically, but they have usually ignored his early stories and have discussed some others only as they have appeared between the publications of the novels. Such treatment has tended to minimize Algren's considerable achievement in the genre: he has written more than fifty substantial short stories, including his first work, during his career as novelist, poet, reviewer, and travel-book writer.

Algren considered the short story important. In 1945, when he decided to settle in Chicago and to become "serious about writing," he concentrated on the short stories which were included in his only collection of the genre, *The Neon Wilderness*. A number of his short stories, little altered, have become episodes in the novels; a number of episodes from the novels, just as slightly changed, have been published separately as short stories. Algren admits, in fact, that the only way he knows to write a novel is "just to keep making it longer and longer."[1] These tendencies suggest that, in some important ways, the short stories rather than the novels might be a clearer index to Algren's talent.

I *The Beginning: "So Help Me"*

Algren's first short story, "So Help Me," is an extended dramatic monologue, a precursor of the highly charged interrogation scenes containing the long and often subtle confessionals which become some of the most effective sections in Algren's later work. In "So Help Me," the speaker-narrator is a somewhat garrulous, un-educated young man. A Depression-era roustabout, he tells his story, after having been apprehended for murder, as a deposition to a "big-league lawyer." The story he tells is a straight-line and uncomplicated one: Homer, the speaker, tells of seeing a lost-looking but well-dressed Jewish boy, David, standing with a suitcase on a New Orleans wharf, of befriending him in hopes of getting some of his money, of their chance meeting with an ex-convict named Fort in a hobo jungle, of the trio's migrant jobs while Homer and Fort slyly try to con David out of his possessions, and of the actual robbing of the Jitney Jungle store in Texas and the subsequent flight, which is successful until Fort is so panicked by one of David's screaming nightmares that he shoots him.

The story-telling is immature in many ways. Though the monologue form is required perhaps because of the deposition frame and because it is useful for sustaining the character of the speaker, dialogue seems essential in some sections as the story develops; and its avoidance suggests the author's lack of technique or control. Sometimes, too, the almost breathless panoramic paragraphs are broad narratives that hurry the reader across seemingly unnecessary movements and incidents. "So Help Me," however, is a remarkable first story and a foretaste of much that is to become important in Algren's later fiction.

The story's overtone, its density of implication, its texture, and its solidity of detail are noteworthy. The recurrent phrase "so help me" — which appears at least twice at crucial moments during Homer's recounting of the events leading to the impulsive shooting, and again as the last line of the narrative — becomes both a desperate avowal of Homer's sincerity and a plea for assistance. From time to time, Homer unwittingly reveals that he is pathetically unaware of his own obsessions or twisted values, as when, after Homer tricks David into pawning the suitcase until money comes from Homer's mythical brother in Apalachicola, Homer refuses to let Fort accompany him to the pawnshop because his friend "has very deceptive ways sometimes." Moreover, Algren's use of the key phrase "We're cut apart — cut apart!," one which David screams in his walking nightmares, is particularly effective; for it gradually increases the tension until the outcry trips the trigger-finger of the unnerved Fort, and it serves as a recurrent thematic statement of the psychological and spiritual isolation of the characters themselves.

Between "So Help Me" and his collection of short stories, *The Neon Wilderness*, Algren had written his two earliest novels, *Somebody in Boots* and *Never Come Morning*. The first novel was unsuccessful; the second, successful enough to be encouraging without being a best-seller. But, by the author's own admission, he had written both novels during a long period of random, youthful, and largely rootless wandering and army service. By 1945, convinced that, if his writing were to be taken seriously, he had to become serious about writing, he began work on his volume of short stories, only a few of which he had written previously. In his Preface to the American Century Series Edition of *The Neon Wilderness* (1960), he suggests that he was aware that he was herding his career into a new direction: "I made a U-turn in 1946 and ran down several memories I had been haunting before they could start haunting me." These memories were a composite of all his experiences — real, literary, and imaginary.

II *"Design for Departure" and the Jungle Motif*

One of the first and most revealing lessons Algren learned was the difference between the ultra-conscious, the laboriously researched, the over-planned story, and the "accidental" product of his spontaneity and his already fully stocked warehouse of key-phrases, character traits, and informing motifs. Two of the stories in *The Neon Wilderness*, in particular, demonstrate the superiority of Algren's "accidental" story over the "self-conscious" one. "Design for Departure," the principal thematic story of the collection, emphasizes the jungle motif and contains the phrase "the neon wilderness" as part of its narrative. It was carefully researched and "self-conscious." The accidental story, which is one of the real triumphs in Algren's career, is "How the Devil Came Down Division Street."

No writer was ever more determined to make all the "standard" preparations for creating a short story masterpiece than was Algren from the moment he began planning "Design for Departure":

I had a very ambitious hope of writing a really great story, and I went about that in a very determined way. I slept in bum hotels and talked to prostitutes, and I knocked around State and Harrison Streets, tried to hear conversations going on in the next room — picked up, you know, bits of actual conversation. I worked very hard on that. I worked on it off and on for years. That was to be such a great story. Nobody wanted to publish it.

"Design for Departure," which was originally intended as the title for the whole collection, bears a marked resemblance to Stephen Crane's short novel *Maggie: A Girl of the Streets* (1893). The similarity between the two stories is particularly remarkable in the early scenes of "Design for Departure" where the young girl, Mary, blossoms in an environment similar to that which spawned Crane's Maggie; and Mary blossoms there despite what Crane would have called "lurid altercations" between her drunken guardians — her real father, Sharkey, and his common-law wife, the "dead-picker" widow, who exist in avid mutual destructiveness. But, unlike her predecessor, Mary is not that "most rare and wonderful production of a tenement district, a pretty girl," but a blemished one, for her face has a birthmark.

Though Mary's tenement world is not quite the purgatory of Maggie's, it has the more modern trappings of the same dungheap: "Kleenex, fifty-cent horse tickets, and cigarette snipes . . . stamped and trampled into the floor's ancient cracks," a subterranean cave like Crane's "dark region," where she "screamed in sleep without waking at all: as though the fear she felt in her dream was less than the fear she would know upon waking."

These similarities are not surprising since Algren has frequently acknowledged his debt to Crane, once saying "I know him so well I sometimes think I wrote him myself." Parallels with other Naturalist pioneers, particularly with Dreiser's *Sister Carrie*, would be easy to make; but such comparisons tend to diminish a talent whose strengths are more unique than derivative. The "work-monotony" syndrome of Naturalist fiction, for instance, could be traced to Emile Zola, but is a too unavoidable observation of life to charge authors with borrowing it from one another. The kindred monotonies of the sewing-machine jobs of Dreiser's Carrie and Crane's Maggie, the packing-house jobs of Upton Sinclair's Jurgis Rudkus in *The Jungle*, and the bacon-wrapping job of Algren's Mary are all manifestations of a universal condition more than of a literary convention.

In "Design for Departure," the time comes when Mary moves away from Sharkey and from the widow's proud boast, "Sometimes I fall down. But I don't stagger." Alone in the dreadful, impersonal isolation of "one of those cheap caverns which are half way between a rooming house and a cheap hotel," Mary becomes an automaton at her bacon-wrapping job and otherwise occupies "a twilit land between sleep and waking" — always sleeping in the foetal position as an envelope against the void of her life. Into this vacuum comes deaf Christiano, the sweeper of halls, who waits in Mary's room to seduce her; and she succumbs with only a whimper. After she has become a partner in the badger game with Christy and Ryan, the proprietor of the Jungle Club, a victim calls the police, who take

Christy, "the one human being who had been kind to her," away in handcuffs. During his imprisonment, Mary turns to prostitution and drug addiction, and becomes diseased. When Christy returns, she warns him away, performing in her disease and despair the inevitably appropriate act demanded by circumstance — the request that Christy give her the last, lethal dose of narcotics to ease them both from a life become irrevocably intolerable.

With the appearance of deaf Christiano the uniqueness of Algren's jungle world becomes unmistakable; it is no longer the same as Crane's or Dreiser's. Mary is not, like Maggie, "pounced upon by the first wolf in this jungle and seduced."[2] Instead, both Mary and Christy are victims of psychological and spiritual starvation. She is seduced by a deeply flawed jungle humanoid whose very incompleteness helps to explain, within the only framework possible to those who must survive in a jungle metropolis, not only his capacity for true if primitive kindness but also his ultimate fidelity to her. And, by the same token, Mary's only resistance is the whimper of one who, knowing nothing but defeat, must accept her seduction as the established pattern of her existence.

But even in Algren's special universe of crime, prostitution, drunkenness, and drug addiction, Mary finds with Christy the only human rapport she has ever known — in its way a genuine love which exists independent of all that is otherwise sordid and degraded. With Christy's imprisonment, however, all hope disappears. In her narcotic degeneracy and disease, she counts it an act of Christian mercy that Christy will, on his return, perform the last narcotic ritual necessary to round out the "elaborate preparation for death"[3] which has been her life.

With the infusion of human sensibility and Christian mythos into the jungle world, Algren achieves a trademark of his contribution to American Naturalistic fiction: deep compassion for the fallen and degraded.[4] In this story, Algren makes his most obvious excursion into Christian allegory; for he makes Christy a half-brother to those pseudonyms of Christ produced by Joseph Conrad, Fyodor Dostoevsky, Ivan Turgenev, Faulkner, Albert Camus, and Hemingway.[5] Though somewhat inverted, the allegory is plain not only in the names of Mary and Christy themselves but also in Mary's search for deliverance from a lost world through the sacrificial act of a mortal Christ. The Christian mythos, a symptom of unremitting seriousness in Algren's early work, is perhaps too weighty for the basic subject matter in "Design for Departure." Nonetheless, perceptive critics like George Bluestone have recognized it as one of the most admirable stories in the collection.

III "How the Devil Came Down Division Street"

Part of the lesson which Algren learned from writing "Design for Departure" was that he could not immerse himself too early and too painstakingly in serious preparation without stifling life-giving properties which a greater reliance upon intuition could preserve. The value of the lesson has been proved by the continued popularity of a story which he wrote in one afternoon and revised only once, a basically serious study of Division Street life told with the bizarre lightness of much of his best work since that time. Needing some money in a hurry, Algren fictionized a Pole's account of a neighborhood family that was convinced that its house was haunted. The result was "How the Devil Came Down Division Street," a story which "is still brand new," though so often anthologized (even in foreign languages) that Algren now denies reprint permission since he fears its over-publication.

The narrative begins as a frame story in which Roman Orlov accepts a double-shot of whiskey from the narrator in return for an explanation of how he became the acknowledged prince of Division Street drunks. The immediate scene is the Polonia Bar on Division Street where Roman spends his life declaring that "The devil lives in a double-shot" and pleading with his friends to help him "drown the worm" which, though drowned each day, nonetheless gnaws incessantly. Long in the telling, broken by curses and sobs, Roman's tale is founded upon a narrative irony in which the miraculous saving of a totally derelict drunken father creates a totally derelict drunken son.

The machinery by which Algren achieves this switching of positions appears slight and perhaps too ingenious at first glance; but, viewed in environmental terms, it is ultimately defensible: one of the crucial conditions of the family's existence is sleeping accommodations which force one or another of the family to sleep under rather than in a bed. Papa Orlov, in whose head "many strange things went on," earns pennies at night by playing his accordion in Division Street taverns. By day, he sleeps in the tenement apartment, but never in Mama O's bed. It is as though, "having given himself all night to his accordion, he must remain true to it during the day." The apartment contains only two beds — one is for eleven-year-old Teresa and Mama Orlov, who "cooked in a Division Street restaurant by day and cooked in her own home at night"; the other bed is shared by thirteen-year-old Roman and the seven-year-old twins. Slumber is so precarious that "nobody encouraged Papa O. to come home at all"; but, when he does, he sleeps under Roman's bed until the children go to morning Mass.

The problem is a simple one of domestic geometry. And, since the solution works, there is no difficulty until the terms of the problem require substitutions. Trouble begins when the family is upset by a ghostly knocking at the door: first, on a Sunday with only Papa O. at home; again, that evening; again, in the middle of the night. A dream of a blood-spattered young man waiting in the hall convinces Mama O. that some change is coming; therefore, she is not surprised when Papa O. comes home inexplicably without his accordion. Implored for an explanation of the knocking and the dream, neighbors tell of the brutal murder there in which a young man crazed by drink had beaten to death his unwed mate and had then hanged himself in the closet. They had been buried together in un-sanctified ground, and he is now returning in search of peace.

The priest proclaims it the "will of God that the Orlovs were chosen to redeem the young man through prayer and that Papa O. should have a wife instead of an accordion." So, deprived of an ac-cordion through God's will, Papa stays home, sleeps in his proper place beside Mama, and soon becomes the best janitor on Noble Street. As a result, the haunting ceases. By and large, this miracle saves the Orlov family; it brings from the landlord a surcease of rent and makes the previously retarded Teresa the most important person in her class. But for Roman, the miracle is only that of the change-ling; for, with Papa sleeping in Mama's bed, Teresa must take Roman's place beneath the bed. Unable to sleep there at night, Roman haunts Papa's well-worn paths to the taverns to drown the worm each night until that bitterest hour, dawn, when "he must go home though he has no home." That is why, as the biggest drunk on Division Street, Roman insists that the devil lives in a double-shot.

In "How the Devil Came Down Division Street" Algren added a dimension which characterizes most of his later work: the bizarre, flamboyant, and sometimes grim humor. And nowhere has he more successfully combined the elements of the modern gothic, the comic ghost story, and meaningful social commentary.

IV *Dramatized Sketches: Three Interrogation Stories*

The charge most frequently leveled against Algren's short fiction is that it consists of sketches rather than of fully formed short stories. He concentrated upon what Bluestone calls moments of "frozen

change before a death or final loss"[6] which characterize passages in
the early novels, especially in *Never Come Morning*. Most of
Algren's short fiction substitutes for conventional rounding-out of
action a deliberately static framework in which the very lack of action emphasizes the paralysis of characters who must be brought to
the full realization of their paralysis, as in the last line of "A Bottle of
Milk for Mother" — "I knew I'd never get to be twenty-one
anyhow."

"A Bottle of Milk for Mother" is the most widely anthologized of
three dramatized sketches which are among Algren's most effective
contributions to modern short-story craft: the "interrogation
stories." Some of these are elaborate verbal exchanges drawn from
official police "line-ups"; others are more fully narrated adaptations
of the "third degree." At some time between 1935 and 1941, in an
attempt to recover a stolen wallet, Algren received a card admitting
him to regular police line-ups. For years thereafter he haunted these
ceremonials where he observed, absorbed, and learned to interpret
stance, glance, gesture, facial and auditory inflection, and the dialec-
tal thrust typical of reactions between accuser and accused.

The respect and popularity accorded "A Bottle of Milk for
Mother" are the result of the directness and penetration with which
Algren manages a verbal duel between a suspect and a police captain. The young Polish baseball-pitcher-turned-prize-fighter, Bruno
"Lefty" Bicek, possesses slow-witted street cunning. The precinct
police captain Kozak (called Tenczara in *Never Come Morning*) is
an omniscient nemesis figure whose weary cynicism camouflages an
intimate knowledge of the criminal mind and a solid expertise in the
ploys of interrogative suggestion, innuendo, and snare. From the
beginning, the game is hopeless for the cornered suspect; but in the
long run, Captain Kozak proves himself even the better gambler.

The story opens in Captain Kozak's office into which Bruno,
charged with the fatal robbery-shooting of an old man in a tenement
hallway, is ushered by Sergeant Adamovitch. With dramatic irony,
the opening sentence tells the reader something Bruno himself does
not know: this is his "final difficulty" with the police. From the moment Bruno enters, he is subjected to the expert terrorizing of the official team composed of two sergeants, a plain-clothes man, and a
reporter. The story is an advanced form of the deposition, but the
unbroken monologue of "So Help Me" becomes in this story an
elaborate pattern of move and countermove, one always controlled
by the cynical though sphinx-like captain, and one always edging the

suspect inexorably toward final revelations which he does not know
he is making.

The crucial turns are often very delicate, as when Kozak virtually
ignores the pathetically naive alibi that Bruno was only on an errand
to get a bottle of milk for his mother, or when Bruno is rattled by
Kozak's abrupt shift from the familiar "Lefty" to the austere and
threatening "Bicek." Each time the suspect feels that he has
managed to gloss his own portrait, he finds it looking more and more
like a prison photo. Finally, on his knees in a cell in an accidental attitude of prayer as he looks for his pavement-colored cap, he mutters
to impersonal walls, "I knew I'd never get to be twenty-one
anyhow."

Captain One-Eye Tenczara of *Never Come Morning* is the first of
Algren's weary, burdened, but sardonic and wily cops. After
conducting the interrogation which is the basis of "A Bottle of Milk
for Mother," Tenczara also presides over the first important line-up
scene in Algren's stories, a scene which is the progenitor of "The
Captain Has Bad Dreams," which in turn became the germinal idea
for "The Captain Is Impaled." In this evolution lies one of the
remarkable paradoxes in Algren's fiction: for a writer both
celebrated and condemned for his sympathy with the underdog, the
downbeaten, the oppressed and cornered, Algren has shown a surprising sympathy with the haunted and spiritually oppressed law officer.

The interrogation stories reveal the development of this broader
recognition in Algren's writing. At first, with One-Eye Tenczara's interrogations, the focus is upon the criminal and the crime. The officer's function is largely that of a medium through which the reader
can perceive the complexity of the sub-legal, sub-social, sometimes
even sub-human activities which persist behind the city's respectable façades. But from story to story, as lost soul follows lost soul
across a platform under spotlights, the focus shifts from the accused
to the accuser. The guilt of the criminal becomes, at last, that of the
oppressor also.

Together, the stories "The Captain Has Bad Dreams" and "The
Captain Is Impaled" serve as the final stages in this evolution; but
the difference lies chiefly in the greater intensity with which the
later story shifts guilt to the interrogator. These veteran police cap-
tains with at least eleven years' service are jaded, disillusioned,
hardened officers — ones as hard as the hardened criminals they in-
terrogate interminably. Haunted by the creeping erosion of their

rightness and assurance, they become at last compassionate in their cynicism; identifiable with those they oppress, they are cognizant that they, too, are implicitly guilty of the wrongs they condemn eternally in others.

Both stories share the same subject, one that is perhaps best capsulized by Algren himself in a passage from "The Captain Is Impaled," in which he tells whom the "snickerers" are waiting in the darkened auditorium to identify: "the man who'd slugged the night watchman and the one who'd snatched the imported purse through the window of the Moving El; for him who'd chased somebody's sister down a dead-end alley or forged her daddy's signature; tapped a gas main or pulled a firebox; slit the janitor's throat in a coal-bin or performed a casual abortion on the landlord's wife in lieu of the rent." Others are also there, to be identified or charged not by the victimized public but by the police themselves. Like spirits in a latter-day *Divine Comedy*, these are malefactors who do violence not upon others but upon themselves — the drunks, hop-heads, loiterers, attempted suicides.

The setting is minimal in "The Captain Has Bad Dreams": "They come off the streets for a night or a week and pause before the amplifier with a single light, like a vigil light, burning high overhead. Each pauses, one passing moment, to make his brief confessional." Though essentially the same, the setting is elaborated upon in "The Captain Is Impaled" in which the time is "that loneliest of all jailhouse hours, the hour between the evening chow-cart's passing and Lights On." The reader is with the prisoners in a jail cell, and the auditorium is "just the other side of that green steel door." Furthermore, the reader is painfully aware that those who lurk nightly in the dark auditorium are now coming in. These are the "snickerers," who come every night to point their fingers at the accused, even though the accused can admit no fear. Everybody is "in on a bad rap. So how could anyone get fingered?"

In "The Captain Has Bad Dreams," the identification of the accuser with the sufferers is vague. Some nights the captain "was all for hanging the lot of them at 11 P.M. On other evenings he advised them to take turns throwing themselves under the El, which roared regularly past." But at home he is plagued by dreams with mystic overtones — dreams in which "they passed and repassed him restlessly, their faces half averted, forever smiling uneasily as though sharing some secret and comforting knowledge of evil which he could never know." The lost ones have given him his own cross; and, like them, he is impaled upon it. The impalement image itself, when it first occurs in "The Captain Has Bad Dreams," applies not to the captain but to an addict who has given himself up voluntarily and stands against the lighted wall "as though impaled, an agonized Jesus in long-outgrown clothes."

By the time "The Captain Is Impaled" appeared, two years later, Algren had transfered the impalement from the tortured addict to the tortured captain. Though the story is only an episode in the career of Frankie Machine in *The Man with the Golden Arm*, it is a satisfactory short story which achieves fullest irony and mature thematic force. Understanding the indictment leveled at him by a defrocked priest, "We are all members of one another," the captain watches the "snickerers" leave the line-up room; but he stays behind with his prisoners "to follow each man to a cell all his own, there to confess the thousand sins he had committed in his heart . . . for there was no priest to wash clean the guilt of the captain's darkening spirit nor any judge to hear his accusing heart." He warns himself to come off his own cross, but he cannot, for "the Captain was impaled."

V *Sagas of Organized Stumbling*

Algren's stories are highly homogeneous. As has been noted, his subjects are dope addiction, prostitution, incarceration, gambling, prize-fighting, horse racing, and army life, one or more of which predictably appears in most of his work. Nonetheless, certain stories have similarities which differentiate them from others. Three, for instance, are related to the interrogation group because they deal with conditions which drive suspects into police offices or line-ups and because they reflect the value-deterioration and the rationalizing of the confessionals.

"Poor Man's Pennies" is built almost entirely upon the "transparent alibi" typical of the line-up confessionals. Here the alibis help create a narrative that explores the reasons for a nice girl's involvement with a worthless fabricator. Gladys, understanding that Rudy's compulsive lies "are a poor man's pennies," manages to marry him to get him paroled to her; and she spends ten trouble-free years in probationary bliss. "Poor Man's Pennies" has moments of broad farce or even burlesque, and it ends in at least temporary salvation; but it is, nevertheless, "a saga of organized stumbling by born incompetents toward a palpably impossible end."[7]

The other two stories of this group, "A Lot You Got to Holler" and "Please Don't Talk About Me When I'm Gone," are more serious sagas of organized stumbling; both are told in first person as forms of the confessional. The first story is an indictment of a brutal, unfeeling father who deprives his son of his mother, marries the mother's sister, and punishes the boy indiscriminately for becoming an inveterate thief and con-boy. Searching for the lost warmth of his mother and adopting all forms of subterfuge because of his fear of his father, the boy finds himself in a fierce paternal feud. Like Huckleberry Finn, he ponders the morality of adult society; he finds its values so inverted that he concludes "I was always in the clear so long as I was truly guilty. But the minute my motives were honest someone would finger me." The story is a handbook of petty thievery, short-change artistry, and con-methods through which the boy progresses until he is jailed and then paroled to his father, whom he baits until the old man is glad to be rid of him.

"Please Don't Talk About Me When I'm Gone," a somewhat rambling story, begins at the moment when Rose, a prostitute who is arrested for murder, is ushered into the police wagon. As the crowd pulls back, she thinks, "My whole life it's the first time anyone made room for me. And now just look what for." Told in retrospect, the story ends at the same moment and with the same words.

VI *Legal Retribution: Imprisonment and Release*

Clearly related to the stealing, con-game, and interrogation stories is another three-tale cluster representing the legal retribution which society imposes upon the caught and convicted. These stories, identifiable as studies of incarceration and release, explore in turn early confinement in a juvenile detention home, adult confinement in a southern jail, and the disillusionment of release. "The Children" is a devastating treatment of the stupidity of professional "do-gooders" who smugly minister to budding hoods without the remotest perception of what is happening inside their heads. The detention home or "reformatory" does no reforming but serves as a centralized criminal-information exchange where the inmates' appearance of docility toward over-dressed women benefactors is their cover for an esoteric underworld education.

"El Presidente de Méjico," an adaptation of the Texas jailhouse episode in *Somebody in Boots*,[8] is the most effective of the "tank stories." Though the title focuses attention upon Portillo the Mexican, a six-week bridegroom with a pregnant wife, the story really concerns the jailhouse world in which a young man learns the world's cruelties. Portillo, detained for questioning about the location of a still, is kept outside the cell-block to protect him from Jesse Gleason, the "bad-man" of the tank. Gleason, who had killed Mexicans on both sides of the border, had returned for justice to the American side where "he had more relatives than the sheriff and was confident of beating the rap." Without explanation, Portillo is released; but he is dragged back at nightfall with a great bullet hole in his stomach, a result of his having tried to run from the sheriff. Too nearly dead to be able to grant permission for surgery, he dies on the floor, never to know whether his unborn son becomes President of Mexico. Later, after Gleason is acquitted, he is endowed with Spanish boots and Portillo's sombrero.

Slight but poignant, "The Brother's House" probes into that overwhelming longing for release which all prisoners must outlast. David survives by dreaming of his return to the house where he had lived with his brothers. The beatings they gave him cannot be admitted into his dreams; he has nowhere else to go. Released, he trudges homeward for eighteen days, only to be met at the gate with the query, "What do you want?"

VII *Gambling Tales*

Two stories, "Stickman's Laughter" and "Katz," concern loss by gambling. In both stories, the losing-formula is classic and the same: a mounting pile of winnings, then suddenly — nothing. "Stickman's Laughter," however, has one of the few near-redemptive conclusions in all of Algren's fiction. Like the good husband he is, Banty Longobardi takes his pay home to an equally good wife who, though rarely away, has not returned from visiting her mother. Lonely and disappointed, Banty resorts to a crap game; wins forty dollars; and, even more bitterly disappointed when his wife is not yet home to share his good fortune, gets drunk and loses all his money at the same crap table. Ashamed and fearful, he goes home again and finds his wife willing to take blame for being away and even to sympathize with "poor Banty" for missing dinner and the movies. "So nothing important had been lost after all."

Such a salvation is impossible for Katz, the young poker player whose name is the title of his story. With sixty-five dollars in his pocket, he runs the win-then-lose route until he has only eight quarters left. In a five-dollar-start game, he pretends to have more in a closed fist and calls that he has "threes" to make the dealer think he has three threes instead of two. He is caught and thrown down the stairs in disgrace. Unlike Banty, who gambles only from loneliness, Katz feels that money makes him important, invincible: "Katz believed in lucky bucks, fast money, and good women." His defeat is ignominious; his character makes it impossible for him to know the redeeming love to which Banty returns.

In both stories, much depends upon the ironic twists of the parrot-like cry of stickman and dealer, "Tell 'em where you got it and how easy it was." The cry has a literal meaning when Banty wins but an ironic one when he loses; it is ironic on one level when Katz loses the first time; but, as a sneering phrase directed at an inept cheater, it means something altogether different the second time.

VIII   *Prostitution, Drug Addiction, and Prize Fighting*

As concrete and authoritative as the gambling tales but even more sordid and hopeless in outlook are several stories dealing with prostitution and drug addiction. The slightest of the group, "Is Your Name Joe?," is the half-demented monologue of a simple-minded prostitute to whom all men are "Joe" because "Joes" have been the only ones important enough in her life to drive her steadily into perdition. Two other stories, written in the late 1960's, return to the successful addiction-prostitution themes of the two major novels. "All Through the Night" probes once more the faith which the prostitute has in the "Daddy" whose only real aim is to gain all he can from her. As a graphic revisitation to the addict world of *The Man with the Golden Arm*, the story is effective; but the use of names with biblical vibrations, Beth-Mary and Christian, is not as well integrated with the thematic values as in "Design for Departure."

In "Decline & Fall of Dingdong-Daddyland" (1969), Algren amplifies the kitchen condom-factory episode from *A Walk on the Wild Side*. Essentially a story of mutual entrapment in which an old ex-con provides the heroin for two addicted ex-hookers in return for their help in manufacturing garish condoms, Dingdong Daddies and their variations, it is a terrifying tale despite the gloss of broad humor with which it is told. These derelicts exist in hateful interdependence until the old man dies, leaving a hundred-thousand dollars worth of heroin in the brass bedposts, where it remains to this day safe and dry in some forgotten dump underneath an El.

Two stories in *The Neon Wilderness* are only peripherally prostitution stories. "Kingdom City to Cairo" is a first-person story told by a young hitch-hiker picked up by a former Seventh-Day Adventist minister. The minister has been deprived of his credentials for making a bawdy house of an historic hotel he owns in a neighboring town, where he also goes to pick up mail from his brother's wife with whom he is having an affair. He keeps telling the young man, "You see, I have a weakness"; but, even after the young man accepts a free bed and escapes an army of bed-bugs in the ancient bawdy house, he is still unsure "whether the Reverend's weakness was women, whisky, his single kidney, or practical joking."

A more substantial prostitution-prize-fighting tale, "Depend on Aunt Elly," is one of the most ironically bitter stories in *The Neon Wilderness*. In addition to developing the theme that a girl can never escape prostitution after she has adopted the profession, the story also successfully combines Algren's interest in official graft, entrapment, incarceration, and prize fighting. The title, lifted from the context, is biting in its implications: "Aunt" turns out to be a proprietary rather than a familial term, and Elly herself is truly dependable but only in collecting a monthly fee from Wilma, the small-time prostitute, whom she had bilked into spending all of her money to buy a furlough instead of the promised commutation from the prison farm. A part-Indian prize fighter, Baby Needles, rescues Wilma from a whorehouse, marries her unaware of her perpetual debt to Elly, derives from the marriage courage to develop his "bolo punch" into near-championship form, but then finds and reads one of Elly's dunning letters, loses heart, returns to liquor, and rejects his wife for not being honest with him. He is left alone with only Wilma's lucky-piece, a pathetic rabbit's foot, that is "clutched in his hand, the great knuckles showing white and helplessly through the copper skin." Altogether, the story is one of Algren's most effective efforts to depict the luckless, accidental fashion in which desperate people are deprived of mutually redeeming love.

Baby Needles is typical of the second- and third-rate prize fighters who appear in Algren's fiction; all of them yearn for fame and money, and sometimes they approach both, but they see them fade mirage-like. This syndrome reaches its lowest depths in *The Neon Wilderness* story "Million-Dollar Brainstorm" where the brainstorm is not the million-dollar one which the mountainous pug Tiny Zion dreams of, but his own literally scrambled brains. After bringing Tiny home from his last knockout and a messy binge, his manager knows by looking at his eyes that Tiny will be throwing his mother out the window next, "Or jumpin' outa it hisself."

Though the prize fight stories always deprive the fighter of fighter's dreams, they sometimes allow him to settle for something else, or even for something more meaningful and permanent. Two progressive phases of such settlement appear in a 1968 *Atlantic* story, "Home to Shawneetown," and in "He Swung and He Missed," which was part of *The Neon Wilderness*. "Home to Shawneetown" is the saga of a better-than-average itinerant fighter who meets and beats good opposition all over the country but who sees clearly in time that a swab stick, a roll of gauze, and a vaseline jar are his total reward for getting his "face punched in for fourteen years." So he accepts his wife's long-standing suggestion that they open a diner, and with the first-night customers he contentedly watches a televised fight between two of his old opponents.

The last of the three prize fight stories, "He Swung and He Missed," reflects Algren's admiration for Hemingway's classic story "Fifty Grand." Though Young Rocco is not championship material, he gives everything to every fight and never considers taking a dive — until the last fight of his career, which he agrees to throw because he cannot stand seeing his wife without decent shoes. But he finds when in the ring that he cannot willingly lose; "his own pride" is "double-crossing him." Solly knocks him out, however — in a prolonged and graphic fight sequence as specific as the best blow-by-blow commentary. In the dressing room, his wife confronts him fearfully, saying she had bet all his advance on him and now they have nothing. But he is able to grin "a wide white grin," and "that was all she needed to know it was okay after all."

IX *Army Life*

Since Algren had little rapport with the manufactured society of military life, his five army stories are not among his best. Though they have all the concreteness and specificity of his other works — intimate knowledge of the mystique behind hierarchies of rank, command of black-market angles, perception of the enlisted man's view of military punishment and reward — the characterizations seldom achieve the keenness of Algren's dope addicts, jailbirds, and prize fighters. In "That's the Way It's Always Been" and in "The Heroes," the real war is not with the Germans but with American officers, both commissioned and "numcum," including the chaplain. The commanding officer, a superb incompetent, devotes his energies to prolonging the war, to delivering marathon lectures, and, like the chaplain, to cornering expensive war souvenirs in the field and nurses in bed. To the plain soldier, even God is a grafter; for His vice-regent the chaplain preserves the profitable status quo with glib wisdom, "That's the way it's always been." The relentless war between enlisted man and commanding officer is a landlubber's *Mr. Roberts* in which a major victory is achieved when the medics have the Colonel himself as a pneumonia patient; and the Mexican-Osage Corporal Hardheart of "The Heroes" is a character not far removed from the half-insane aspect of the military establishment later chronicled by Joseph Heller in *Catch-22*. Many soldiers flee such insanity, as does the Negro soldier of "He Couldn't Boogie-Woogie Worth a Damn," who holes up in Marseilles with a lovely Algerienne prostitute who promises to smuggle him into Africa as her Algerien. The story is interesting partly as an early Marseilles version of *Chicago: City on the Make*, for it penetrates the heart and spirit of the great French industrial metropolis: "a worker's city, a dirty dockside mechanic sprawling, in a drunken sleep, his feet trailing the littered sea."

In "No Man's Laughter," an air-force cousin of *What Makes Sammy Run?*, a young habitual delinquent, who develops into the best "wheelman" on Chicago's Near Northwest Side, becomes an air-force hero by diving his plane into an enemy cruiser because he cannot tolerate imaginary mocking laughter from the decks below. In "Pero Venceremos," a tale of reminiscence, a man wounded during the Spanish war relives the experience incessantly in bars and saloons and bores his friends and acquaintances, most of them veterans of World War II. The pathetic punch-line comes when, after remarking that "it's just like yesterday," the wounded veteran O'Connor shakes his head "like a man recalling an endless dream" and murmurs in self-contradiction, "It feels more like tomorrow."

X *"The Face on the Barroom Floor"*

Algren has produced only one short story which can be legitimately labeled a barroom story, "The Face on the Barroom Floor," one of the most convincing and hard-hitting pieces of fiction in *The Neon Wilderness*. Remarkable for its introduction of the early prototype of Schmidt, the awesome legless man of *A Walk on the Wild Side*, "The Face on the Barroom Floor" successfully communicates the pride and strength of the great torso on a wheeled platform, Railroad Shorty, who even on his wheels can beat anybody at anything. Venus Darling, the little peep-show peeler, boasts of his love-prowess and is offended at the bartender's joke, "Is that where he gets his money then?" Bound to refute the intolerable suggestion that he takes money from women, "Halfy" challenges young Fancy and, at the ghoulish urging of bar patrons, pounds his face "to a scarlet sponge" on the barroom floor, wheels away "like Jesus Christ ridin' his cross," and leaves Brother B. to close his bar forever. The fight is as senseless as the one in Crane's *The Blue Hotel;* but it is more bestial and is given point by the same kind of ironic signs, here NO CREDIT and NO SALE,[9] which make all necessary comment.

XI *Race Track Stories; Mood and Occasional Pieces*

During the 1960's, Algren, a lifelong horseplayer, worked somewhat desultorily on a "racetrack novel." This material supplied a few short stories, such as "The Moon of the Arfy Darfy" and "A Ticket on Skoronski" which appeared in the *Saturday Evening Post* in 1964 and 1966, respectively. "The Moon of the Arfy Darfy" is the first-person account of Floweree, an unlucky jockey who, at the suggestion of a bar proprietor, impersonates the famous jockey Willie Hartack so that a "big-hand, big-belly, big-laugh, old jolly-boy" from Omaha can bribe him to throw a race. With the real Hartack riding, the horse wins as expected; and "It looked like a rainy day in Omaha." Only partly a racing story, "A Ticket on Skoronski" uses a racing dream as extra-sensory prognosticator and mood builder.

Through the 1960's, Algren's short pieces attracted the attention of men's magazines like *Playboy* and *Dude,* a market which has been receptive not only to fiction but also to mood and occasional pieces, adventure, autobiography, and the highly personal essay. Much of Algren's later work falls into these categories, and "God Bless the Lonesome Gas Man" is typical of these later works. Drawing rather lightly upon the army-prize-fighting-barroom materials of previous stories, it is the slight but ingenious tale of Chester, who becomes a "smeller" for the "mighty utility," Some People's Gas. His nose was so often broken during an army boxing career that a necessary operation had given him the olfactory sensitivity of a bloodhound. Night or day he is on call to smell for gas leaks in endless miles of tubing. He is so good at his job that he predicts an explosion where the company has no records of gas lines. But the smell of gas gets into his skin; his cherished wife and his best friends cannot be near him; "he wasn't wanted anywhere but where gas was leaking." He goes to seed and loses weight, but he cannot quit his job because he will get his pension in twenty years.

Among these later efforts are also mood pieces like "The Unacknowledged Champion of Everything" *(Noble Savage,* 1960), autobiographical studies like "The Father and Son Cigar" *(The Playboy Reader)*, and several re-prints of adaptations of sections from *Who Lost an American?* — "Down with All Hands" *(Atlantic* [Dec., 1960]), "The Peseta with the Hole in the Middle" *(Kenyon Review,* Part I [Autumn, 1961]; Part II [Winter, 1962]), and "They're Hiding the Ham on the Pinball King, or, Some Came Stumbling" *(Contact* [Sept., 1961]).

XII *Assessment*

Altogether, the published short stories of Algren are a considerable achievement. Though somewhat uneven, "a curious amalgam,"[10] the stories of *The Neon Wilderness* have elicited unexpected discipline from an author so often charged with looseness and with over-rhapsodizing in his novels. Catherine Meredith Brown justifiably says of the short stories what has rarely if ever been claimed for the novels: "the staccato precision of the writing must be read, remembered, and admired."[11] In contending that Algren "is almost at his best"[12] in the short stories, Maxwell Geismar may have been nearer the truth than many other critics have recognized.

In the short stories, where Algren "can suggest the whole contour of human life in a few terse pages,"[13] he has demonstrated the complete range of his literary attainments. In them was born his distinctive comic sense — the light irony of "How the Devil Came Down Division Street," the satire against mock-respectability in "Kingdom City to Cairo," the broadside against stumbling incompetence in the army stories, and the almost slapstick but sympathetic comedy of "Poor Man's Pennies" — all a prelude to the "Rabelaisian humor" of *A Walk on the Wild Side,* all early evolutionary stages of a comic sense which has dominated Algren's later work.

Nowhere outside the short stories has Algren been so free to exercise his ability to construct a tale from the single, self-revelatory catch-phrase which often becomes the essence of theme: "So help me"; "Sometimes I stagger. But I don't fall down"; "The devil lives in a double-shot"; "I knew I'd never get to be twenty-one anyhow"; "We are all members of one another"; "Lies are a poor man's pennies"; "Tell 'em where you got it and how easy it was"; "I'm the girl that men forget." Nowhere else has he controlled so stringently his tendency to blend the sordid and the poetic; as a result, the short stories have largely escaped the adverse reaction which such a controversial mixture has brought against the novels.

Otherwise, however, the short stories are almost indistinguishable from the novels. In each genre are the same twilit shadow-world of alley, bar, brothel, jail, cave-like tenement, and flea-bag hotel room; the same maudlin and monotonous juke-box tunes punctuated by the rattling of the El above its thousand columns; the same hop-heads, drunks, mackers, outworn prostitutes, sharpies, and general losers; the same grotesqueries of tone and situation; the same concrete and specific insights; the same entrapments, vague unrest, and futile striving. Above all, these stories, despite their shortcomings, are a monument to the honesty, directness, and authority of a writer who has depicted a nightmare society which its parent world would rather disown but which Algren knows too well to let it endure unsung.

CHAPTER 3

Two Final Descendants:
Somebody in Boots *and*
A Walk on the Wild Side

B OTH *Somebody in Boots* and *A Walk on the Wild Side* are founded in the thought and feeling of the early 1930's, and both are products of the literary "cult of experience" of that time. Though two decades and two other novels separate the writing, *A Walk on the Wild Side* is a direct reworking of *Somebody in Boots,* in which Algren had drawn heavily upon his own youthful wanderings from Chicago to New Orleans and back again. Both his first and fourth novels relate the story of the final descendants of "that wild and hardy tribe that had given Jackson and Lincoln birth," as Algren defined the lineage of Cass McKay in a later preface to *Somebody in Boots.*

I Somebody in Boots: *Song of the Road*

Algren begins the narrative of the Linkhorns with the protagonist's father, Stub McKay. Descended from a tribe of free and independent Kentucky hunters, Stub knows himself incapable of adapting to a society which had pressed him and his kind against the Rio Grande, a last asylum, where a man could no longer avoid working with other men if he were to survive and rear a family. Congenitally unprepared for such a world, Stub brawls on Saturday night, sings hymns on Sunday morning, and lives continuously with "The Damned Feeling" of having been tricked and cheated by some unknown, inexorable force. The long line of slaveless yeomen had come at last to a family headed by a stub of a man, "a lean and evil little devil . . . inflammable as sulphur and sour as citron, sullen as a sick steer and savage as a wolf," who is incapable of respect for neighbors or employers, who earns little, and who loses every job by lashing out against those whose orders he must follow.

Stub McKay's destiny is to be destroyed by a civilization with which he is in perpetual and unequal war. After losing his railroad

job because of his "cross-temper," Stub still tries to protect his
"territory"; he prowls the shadows and pursues with hatred each efficient movement of the diminutive Luther Gulliday, who has been
given the railroad job Stub considers his. Maddened by Luther's
methodical steadiness, itself an insult to Stub's incapacity to hold a
job, Stub pounces upon him and shoves him to his death beneath the
wheels of a moving train. When Stub is caught, he is chained in jail
to suffer the retribution which civilization must wreak upon the un-
tamable.

Stub's children — Bryan, Nancy, and Cass — are no better
prepared for adapting to their world than their father was to his.
Bryan, the elder son, who had "left his health in France," is
perpetually half-crazed with drink and spends much of his time with
Mexican prostitutes in rooms behind the pool-hall until his father
beats him to a bloody mush on the cabin floor. Cass, the younger
son, flees in terror, determined to pursue peace and happiness in
other parts of the country.

Somebody in Boots, then, traces the wanderings of the final
McKay descendant, who is in search of his place in the depression
society where even long-established social and economic groups are
uncertain of their niche. From Great-Snake Mountain, Texas, he
hoboes through Southern Texas to New Orleans and back home
again, traveling much of the time with his first bindlestiff side-kick,
the worldly thirteen-year-old Thomas Clay. He encounters old army
men, louse-runners, overbearing Negro attendants, and small-time
whores managed by violent pimps, one of whom marks him permanently with a gray, ribbon-like scar that falls from the corner of
his mouth.

A second passage takes him all over the country, landing him
briefly in Chicago, whence he returns again via Louisiana and East
Texas. Along the way he learns the desperate ploys of panhandler
and con-man, copes with homosexual and railroad bull, participates
in the gang-rape of a Negro woman, and fails in a private attempt to
rape a white girl. He acquires a veteran hobo mentor in the harelipped Olin Jones, gags on the inedible slop dispensed by mission
soup-kitchens, watches a woman in a boxcar give birth to a dead
child, and accepts the friendship of the Negro boy Matches. He is
arrested and serves a nightmare ninety days in the El Paso County
jail where he encounters a fellow prisoner, Nubby O'Neill, the
judge, jury, and executioner of the cell-block kangaroo court.

On a third and last excursion from Great-Snake Mountain, Cass goes directly to Chicago with Nubby, meeting there the passive, mercenary Swedish dance-hall girl, Signe, as well as the ex-seamstress, ex-burlesque dancer and hay-bag prostitute, Norah Egan, whom he takes as mistress and supports by forty-dollar robberies until he is caught and thrown into Cook County Jail. After his sentence is served, he searches the city for Norah. He takes a job as barker for her old burlesque boss, Herman Hauser; watches the crowds for Norah; and finds her at last, only to have her warn him away because she has contracted venereal disease. Tired of the city, worn out by the hustle of the World's Fair, confused by the doctrinaire Communist and Socialist speeches which he has heard at Washington Park with the Negro burlesque comic Dill Doak, Cass endures a beating from Nubby for "walkin' with a nigger so black he looks like a raincloud comin' down the street." Then, as the book ends, both Cass and Nubby turn again to the open road. They follow the tracks wherever they lead.

The apparently random structure of *Somebody in Boots* is in the tradition of American road stories like Jack London's *The Road* (1907) and John Dos Passos' *The 42nd Parallel* (1930). These vigorous American versions of the older picaresque tale had not received much scholarly attention by the mid-1930's, but they began in America at least as early as the late nineteenth century and can be traced through the "Beat" movement of the 1950's in such novels as Jack Kerouac's *On the Road* (1957) and *The Dharma Bums* (1958). Though critics have given little attention to Algren's contributions to the form, all of *Somebody in Boots* and at least Part One of *A Walk on the Wild Side* belong in this tradition, one that is admirably suited to Algren's aim of writing *Somebody in Boots* on behalf of "those innumerable thousands: the homeless boys of America" to whom he dedicated the novel.

The "road stories" of London, Dos Passos, and Algren are largely sagas of travel on the vast American railway system, with its railroad yard, hobo jungle, and the "Man" or scheduled train from city to city. Thrust out to ride the rails by economic necessity or sheer wanderlust, the bums, tramps, or hoboes[1] of these tales become for the first time a recognized socio-economic literary phenomenon in London's *The Road*, then a political agency in Dos Passos' *The 42nd Parallel*, and subjects of humanitarian document in Algren's *Somebody in Boots*. By the time of Kerouac, these social cast-offs were denizens of the highways rather than of the railways; they were of the middle class rather than of the proletariat; they wandered by choice rather than from necessity; and they sought psychological or spiritual identity rather than rudimentary existence.

In the whole tradition of the vagabond tale, depending as it does upon vagrant wandering, looseness of structure has been a reflection of the rootlessness of the people. Formal balance or meticulous integration would be a hindrance to both theme and purpose. As a representative of such a literary tradition, Algren's tale is more tightly organized than most. Cass McKay's painful emergence from Great-Snake Mountain into a complex, brutal, and foreign world is depicted in three phases of vagabondage. During each, he learns matters of increasing importance about himself and about the society which he must penetrate if he is to survive.

Though his first trip from Great-Snake Mountain to "New Awlins" consumes hardly more than a week, it is of signal importance. During this baptismal excursion, Cass is stripped of all illusions about the romance of the road which he had garnered while listening to the hoboes' tales around campfires in the local trackside "jungle." His life, instead, is one of suffering and bare survival. Moreover, he gains his first awareness of the demands of society when a thirteen-year-old professional tramp teaches him that he must learn the rules — if only to know how to break them. Though an abysmally slow pupil, Cass learns that one pays for whatever he receives: in labor, for a meal at a free soup kitchen; in shame, for a showering and delousing; in money, for even the cheapest whore.

At the end of his first sojourn, he knows the immutable laws which govern his kind: "He had learned that for him, Cass McKay, there was no escape from brutality. He had learned that, for him, there was no asylum from evil or pain or long loneliness. It might be that for others there was something different; but for him lonely pain and lonely evil were all that there was in the whole wide world. The world was a cruel place, all men went alone in it. Each man went alone, no two went together. Those who were strong beat those who were weak."

Home again for summer and spring of 1928-1929, Cass sees that conditions there are really the same as elsewhere. Even in Great-Snake Mountain two young brothers kill each other, and an old man in jail admits as his only wrong the crime which is also Cass's: "I was born in Texas with a hungry gut, an' that was my big mistake." Cass becomes a pimp for the girls at the Poblano Cafe; but, after his father is arrested for murdering Luther Gulliday, Cass again takes to the road; however, he does so this time with more knowledge of his limits and possibilities.

He roams everywhere, for it makes no difference to him where he is. All he can retain is a fleeting montage of the world: "Faces, like fenceposts seen from trains, passed swiftly or slowly and were seen no more. They raced for one moment by, they faded, they changed; they became dim, darkened, or ran blackly in the sun." He works the smallest ploys for survival, sometimes botching the subtle ones like shoplifting, and becomes expert in the fundamentals of lone and secret railroad travel: he learns how to sleep atop a swaying boxcar spine, to hop the cars and debark from them, to elude officials, to skirt all manifest danger. During two months in Chicago in 1930, he formulates a rudimentary philosophy: there is no work for his kind because the world belongs to The Owners, who have no places for the already dispossessed.

Without work, he must still move. He attaches himself — as a journeyman under the tutelage of a master craftsman — to a harelipped hobo named Olin Jones, who first claims Cass's attention by casually throwing a homeless black woman to the ground and inviting a boxcar full of tramps to rape her. From Olin, he learns the art of panhandling; and, with Olin, he attends his first burlesque show, the usual cheap and shoddy performance, which he finds ecstatically beautiful. As Cass sits entranced through performance after performance, Olin leaves in disgust, and Cass never sees him again. Aroused by the routine provocations of the burlesque women, Cass attempts to rape a young women in an alley, only to be shamed away by the discovery that she reminds him of his sister Nancy and that she seems hardly more than ten years old. For the first time, he is confronted with the depravity that, under thin control, is himself.

Back in San Antonio in 1931, Cass survives for two days on two cups of coffee from a soup line, half a loaf of bread, and the heart of a lettuce-head found in garbage cans that are miraculously untouched by the coal oil sprayed by city sanitation crews. Trying to evade railroad bulls near Uvalde City, he hurtles through the top door of a moving boxcar and lands on a woman in the throes of childbirth. With the help of a young Negro boy whom he nicknames Matches, Cass provides all the help his ignorance allows; but he manages only to do everything wrong, including sealing the boxcar. The baby is stillborn. The others manage to escape from the boxcar through sheer luck.

Later, wandering through El Paso with Matches, Cass discovers when both are taken to jail that anyone who walks with a "nigger" in the South is himself considered *prima facie* to be one. But he knows, too, that in jail he will at least be fed and will have a place to lie down. During his ninety days in the El Paso County jail, Cass learns the basic mode of jailhouse life; but, more important, he discovers that all he has learned about life on the outside is concentrated here. The society of prisoners is both a mock-up and a mockery of authoritarianism in society at large.

Captives of their own system as much as of statutory law, the jailbirds of El Paso County jail are like all other prisoners in their fervor to build a pecking order which becomes a travesty of the hated system which has put them there. Cass is totally subject to the laws drafted arbitrarily by the self-appointed "judge" of the cell block, a tough and touchy one-armed man named Nubby O'Neill, who wears Spanish boots, a red Gypsy bandanna, a ten-gallon Stetson, and blue jeans. He looks like "a man who had seen too many Western movies in adolescence." Though he was born in South Chicago, his stump is tattooed "Texas Kid: His Best Arm." Nubby rules the cell block with the casual sadism of the self-proclaimed tyrant; he appoints his own "sheriff" and other lesser officers to "kangaroo" all new arrivals, to flay them with a belt, to commandeer their money and belongings as "fines," and to enforce a hierarchy by which he alone determines the portions of food on their plates.

The first jail episode completes the journeyman phase of Cass's discovery of himself and the world. Released from jail along with Nubby, Cass drifts homeward once more in the hope that, after three years on the road, all the trouble at home will now be over. But all such hope is crushed at once and forever when he comes to the gate at dusk to see the house full of drunken men and to have Nancy mistake him for a prospective customer. "A pahty cost but a dolla'," she says to her brother on the familiar dark path to the house. "Hev y'all got a dolla', fella?"

Cass goes to Chicago with Nubby to capitalize upon an apprenticeship in minor crime. The Chicago section is partly the story of Norah Egan, whose career is typical of the working girls exploited by industry; their lives are turned into night journeys from honest toil through burlesque and prostitution to the lowest levels of society. For Norah, having reached that lowest level of "hay-bag" whore, Cass becomes temporarily a kind of savior, one not far removed from other savior-figures in Algren's fiction.

When Cass first meets Norah, however, he is equally in need of saving. As Nubby's accomplice, he has robbed a meat market and escaped, though he believes that Nubby has been apprehended. The robbery itself is the prototype of all amateurishly planned and executed thefts in Algren's fiction. Nubby, the experienced thug, has persuaded Cass to do the actual breaking, entering, and robbing while he, Nubby, stands watch with a gun in the alley. Once inside the market, Cass is besieged by alien impressions so keen and kaleidoscopic as to destroy an ordinary scale of values. Overwhelmed by the smell of meat, he moves as in a dream; like an automaton, he falls over a pile of sawdust; at the sight of money in the cash register, he behaves like a child, his mind roving inexplicably; then, like a madman, he scoops up the money in handfuls, dropping it, banging his head on the counter, crawling after a dime while full rolls of coins remain in the till; and escaping, straddling the window sill as he leaves, he drops the jimmy, and it clangs like cymbals all the way down the concrete alley. As he runs, he hears Nubby's pistol firing. Hours later he realizes that he has escaped with untold wealth — fifty-five dollars in bills and an inestimable amount in coins.

Having accomplished what seemed for him impossible, Cass is incapable of controlling his new image of himself. He resolves to acquire all those symbols which are his idea of status: he will get himself tattooed; he will find himself an impressive nickname — maybe the "Texas Kid" like Nubby, maybe "Bad-Hat" like his own father. Puffed with his own image as never before, he falls asleep on a bench beside the lake, unaware of the image he presents to a world as indifferent as ever: "Passersby observed a gawky country kid with his knees hunkered up to his cheeks and his eyes almost closed, his hair catching fire-glint in the sun, and his mouth hanging open. October beach flies encircled that hair as though seeking some warmth of its blaze. Flies droned lazily, and Bad-Hat snored. Terror had exhausted the Texas Terror." When Cass awakens, he tapes some bills into his navel, then gets drunk and is spotted by Norah Egan, a "hay-bag" whore, a specialist in rolling helpless drunks.

The moment when Cass awakens in Norah's room is a crux in both their lives. Norah has fallen almost beyond redemption; Cass has lost all but the money taped in his navel; and he fears equally police pursuit and vengeance from Nubby. Neither the fleeing criminal nor the "hay-bagger" can afford to trust the other; yet neither knows any other to trust. From this situation is born the first of many strange but tenacious liaisons in Algren's stories — love affairs and marriages that are cemented more tightly by negative than by positive factors. In this case, the cement is an admitted mutual distrust.

Considering himself now a professional thief, Cass launches a series of minor robberies of cab drivers and drug stores. Norah becomes an active accomplice in the robberies, and they achieve an undeniable admiration and affection for each other. Inevitably, however, a drug-store robbery fails. Norah escapes, but Cass is sent for a term in Cook County jail where he discovers that the prisoner's life is essentially the same everywhere.

Released, Cass feels incomplete without Norah, and he searches the city to find her. Norah's old boss, Herman Hauser of the burlesque theater, gives Cass his first steady job as a vendor of candy, tobacco, and magazines. He works hard and eventually graduates to the position of street-barker, from which vantage point he ceaselessly examines the passing crowd for Norah. Meantime, he makes friends with a sophisticated Negro, who takes him to leftist gatherings in Washington Park and tries to indoctrinate him with leftist views which are meaningless to Cass. It is the time of the great Chicago World's Fair, the Century of Progress, with the socioeconomic hypocrisy of the politicians who promote it. In the confusion of the crowds, Cass finds Norah one day, but she is strangely altered. During his prison term she has been forced by circumstance to return to her former condition, even to sink below it, for she is now diseased. Despite his pleading, she leaves him forever.

Reunited with Nubby, Cass closes the only rewarding phase of the depression-world journey which has so far been his life, and the two dispossessed comrades rejoin all other eternally dispossessed upon the common highway to everywhere and nowhere.

II   *The Superstructure*

Upon thorough examination, Algren's apparently discursive first novel reveals a coherent superstructure imposed upon the traditionally loose sub-structure of the typical road story. Though Cass McKay cannot plan his wanderings, they assume an obvious cyclical pattern. In three cycles, each marking a general advance in the experiential development of Cass McKay, the wanderings radiate outward from Great-Snake Mountain and, except for the last, return home. Within this framework, many smaller designs support the structure of the overall pattern to give the story point and coherence.

Cass's three migrations from Great-Snake Mountain are characterized by increasing climactic force. Primed by the local hoboes' stories of the romance of the road, Cass first leaves home after an explosion of brutality which terminates a long-festering hatred between Bryan and Stub. Innocent of life's horrors, Cass cannot bear the sight of his father viciously kicking the older boy in the groin with a pointed boot-toe, visibly emasculating him. Cass does not remember leaving the house; but "even before he realized precisely where he was he had determined not to return. He had had enough of fighting and blood. He had had enough of cruelty." Finding cruelty everywhere, and unequipped to survive in the great world, he must return home more than once, only to be driven away again by cruelties even more unbearable.

After the first short but nearly fatal New Orleans trip, Cass finds that he must seek as haven and hospital the home which he had determined to leave forever. As a hospital, it serves; as a haven, it is ephemeral. Stub's inexorable movement toward obliteration of self and family is nearing its final stage. That blow falls when Stub heaves Luther Gulliday under the wheels of a passing train, an act so monstrous as to send vengeful mobs storming the McKay shack, which now shelters only the offspring of the local fiend. Even more terrifying to Cass than either the murder or the mob is Nancy's hardening of heart and spirit: "She was looking at him out of her father's eyes, cold and sullen and hostile."

When Nancy warns him to leave for his own safety, he recognizes a mandate for vagabondage far more urgent than the family fight which had earlier seemed to him unsurpassable: "This time there would be no one to turn back to. There would be no place waiting for him now. Neither waiting love nor patient peace nor help for daily shame. No shelter when a night was cold. No running now from loneliness and fear of men; only the pain of being ashamed, and the pain of being alone."

After the wider wanderings of his second passage into the world, Cass turns home from a Texas jail, hoping vaguely that his father's monstrous act and its aftermath might have faded from the town's memory and, more important, that he might find Nancy the true and loving sister of his childhood. Instead, he discovers that Nancy has turned the family home into a house and herself into a common town prostitute, one who solicits men for a dollar.

III   *Love and Guilt Motifs*

The psychological shock of this discovery transcends that of the physical violence which motivated Cass's previous escape. For it is accompanied by a sense of guilt, a strong and pervasive motif which Algren uses in *Somebody in Boots* as well as in the rest of his novels.

Crucial to the character of all Algren's non-heroic heroes is the yearning for a love which, once attained, is destroyed by the hero himself. Henceforth, he cannot forget that by a careless act or thoughtless word he has destroyed the only person who has really cared.

To young Cass McKay, his sister Nancy offers the only love in a life otherwise emotionally and spiritually desolate. A sensitive girl who has been both mother and sister to Cass, Nancy is precipitated into maturity by the shock of her father's murder of Luther Gulliday. When, in that sudden metamorphosis, she whirls upon Cass in the besieged family home, Cass understands "that his father had done some terrible thing, but he didn't know what. . . . He could only see that this was not Nancy at all." Too immature to understand Nancy's bitterness and remoteness, Cass resents her depriving him of the only love he had known. He lashes out with the thoughtless words whose import becomes reality and therefore a burden of guilt which Cass must carry with him everywhere: "Y'all kin go down valley-way like you said wunst, to get yo'self a job in a spik whorehouse in La Feria. There's lots o' houses south of La Feria, sister. Y'all might try it over at the Poblano a spell."

Afterwards, whenever Cass yearns for security, warmth, and comfort, his memory turns to Nancy and to the cruel, unjustified remark which he should not have made. Even the purchased favors of prostitutes remind him of Nancy's selfless love. After he has sought her at home for the last time, only to see that she has indeed become what his words had directed, he searches for the lost values of her affection and tenderness in all other women he meets, never to find them again.

IV   Symbols: Boots, Lilac, and Colors

An equally strong agent of coherence in the novel is a tissue of major and minor symbols. The "boots" whose symbolic function begins with the title is the recurrent symbol of authority. Though Algren finds the title "meaningless" by itself, the image of boots woven into the context helps to sustain the constant view that authority is inescapable on all levels of human relationship, however arbitrary or unjust might be its application. Cass learns on his first rail ride to New Orleans: "There were only two kinds of men wherever you went — the men who wore boots, and the men who ran." Whenever Algren wishes to implant a sense of the inhuman, weapon-like quality of the authority symbol, the toes of the boots are pointed.

Cass McKay sees such boots on the feet of all men who exert any kind of authority over him and others of this kind. His father's boots are symbols of family authority and are eventually the direct agents of Bryan's emasculation. The pointed Spanish boots sported by Nubby O'Neill are the salient symbols of Nubby's private and public image as magistrate of the Texas jail cell block; and, even when free of jail, he keeps them in high polish with a special brown wax. Army recruiters, railroad bulls, law officers, and superior vagabonds are all similarly shod.

Cass moves through life, therefore, with eyes and ears alert for the sight and sound of boots. When he upsets a water cooler while trying to get a drink in New Orleans, the service station attendant literally kicks him out; and he feels "the boot bite in deep, deep at the base of the spine where his father's boot would have bitten." While stealing kerosene at home, he listens in fear "for feet that come swiftly in boots. Feet of the law coming swiftly to strike." Waiting in boxcars, he hears boots clattering faster and faster along the tracks, boots that are "two despisers of small things . . . high-heeled, sharp-pointed, imbedded deeply with spikes." And later he realizes that those very spikes keep their wearers secure atop the wet spines of moving boxcars, from which Cass and his kind slip and fall. Little wonder, then, that the Cass McKay who had grown up barefoot is obsessed with the power and danger vested in those who wear boots. While he is trying to sleep with a dead newborn baby and the dying mother in a sealed boxcar, Cass's brain leaps awake over and over again with the alarm, "Look out! Look out! You'll be getting a boot if you don't look out!"

Recurrent emblems from his boyhood years linger in Cass's memory, particularly the sight and smell of the lilac which grew beside the fence during the springtime of his fifteenth year. With the pervasive "velvet smell" of lilac had come his first awareness of sensuality, and somehow that scent became emblematic of his sister, Nancy. "It came to him on the smell of rain, and he heard the tapping of drops on the roof overhead. Behind a thin curtain he heard his sister's low breathing; and knew she slept with her hair for a pillow." Thereafter, in rain and lilac, Nancy's image is reborn for Cass; and, after he has wounded her with words tantamount to his own spiritual destruction, that image is a reminder of his guilt.

Such common phenomena as colors become equally emblematic. After seeing the body of a boy mangled by a passing train, Cass always associates the dominant colors of the experience with life and death. "Yellow and black, yellow and black: these came, for Cass, before he was grown, to be the colors of sun and blood, the hue of life and the shade of death. To think of living was to see yellow; to see blood was to think of black."

V   *Brutality Images: Mutilation and Decapitation*

Closely allied with this particular group of symbols is a series of mutilation and decapitation images. These episodes of violence may result from either sheer, impersonal accident or the most deliberate brutality. When accidental, as in the case of the mangled remains of a boy beside the railroad track, the living gather helplessly but almost casually to watch a life ebb into the cinders; when deliberate, as in the beatings, rapings, and emasculations, the strong enact the show of jungle supremacy upon the weak. To deprive a living being of a vital physical member is either to destroy him, as when Stub emasculates his son Bryan, or to force a cripple to survive by almost superhuman compensation, as when Nubby O'Neill makes the stub of his amputated arm an awesome leather-covered weapon against men with whole but weaker arms.

The most meaningful of these images, however, are those which sever from the body the organs of sense and control — the fearful decapitation images which confront Cass in times of crisis. Among those who are raiding a coal car at Great-Snake Mountain is a tiny Mexican-Indian girl with a doll buggy. After the train has pulled away, the little girl is found beside the track; her arms are outspread, her fingers hold a crumb of coal, and her severed head is on the other side of the rail. Says Luther Gulliday, "She must of slipped a little."

Even more incomprehensible to Cass than this accidental beheading is Bryan's turning in a motiveless rage upon the old but inoffensive family tomcat, whose head he takes in his hands and in a windmill motion "pops off" the body which streaks Cass with blood in its flight across the room. The decapitation of the cat extends the significance of the earlier decapitation of the little girl and serves as a prelude to later occurrences. When Cass regains consciousness after his first beating in New Orleans, he sees, staring directly at him with ants in its eyesockets, the bodiless head of a dog. When he then discovers the knife wound which marks his face for life, he concludes that "the devils had tried to cut his throat."

All such images are directly related to a vital query which gives Cass an early sense of imminent death and which lurks unanswered in his mind throughout the story: "Was this all that poor people did? Did everyone, everything, cats and hawks and men and women —

did all of these live only to eat, fight and die . . . ? It seemed to him then that in being a man there might be something more." The constantly integrated emblems of boots, colors, odors, and forms of violence create a pattern which not only answers Cass's question but also makes *Somebody in Boots* a more coherent "road story" than most of its kind.

VI   *Stylistic Blend: Naturalism, Lyricism, and Diatribe*

Unflinching in his painting of the sordid, the violent, and the indifferent, Algren is unafraid to balance the Naturalist view with a probing of the delicacy and the aspiration of the individual human spirit. In *Somebody in Boots,* he makes his first attempt to accomplish this precarious stylistic blend. Cass McKay, though born into a graphically depicted world of poverty, dispossession, and brutality, brings into that world an almost Wordsworthian sense of intimations of immortality: "A sudden light would flash within his brain illuminating earth and sky — a common bush would become a glory, a careless sparrow on a swinging bough a wonder to behold." Almost invariably the lyricism of such passages serves as a counterpoint to the hard-bitten prose, one affirming rather than denying the Naturalist's stance. Sometimes Algren creates a single paragraph combining the two:

> Then such dreams as he would have! Once he was atop the utmost peak of the highest mountain on earth, clouds and storm winds breaking about him, snow-gales sweeping down. . . . And everything was so wild and strong that when he awoke in the morning he was sickened by the sights and sounds and smells of the house: the stains of Stubby's spittle and Bryan's cut-plug tobacco juice dried in brown globs against the wall; the sweaty, yellowish smell of unclean bedclothes beneath him, and the sour smells from the kitchen.

The hard, crusty tone of the Realistic detail remains always in Algren's prose, for it is useful whatever the locale. In his first novel, however, the lyric tone is confined almost entirely to the close-to-nature rural scenes and to the impressionable boyhood years of Cass McKay. Later, in the Chicago novels, the lyric tone is transferred to the concrete and steel of the great city and to the mature sensibility of his characters.

A clue to Algren's lyric sense is his penchant for imbedding in the context quotations from songs of many kinds: American and Spanish folk songs, hobo ballads, jailhouse ditties, blues, popular love songs. Sometimes the song fragments fit the prevailing mood, sometimes they serve as a memory-teaser, and sometimes they initiate a series of actions.

At the other end of the stylistic spectrum in *Somebody in Boots*, however, is a strangely polemical section — almost a separate set-piece at the beginning of Part Four — which is a diatribe against World's Fair opulence in a city beset by poverty and social inequality. Here, Algren openly directs his anger against the smugly ignorant assurance of politicians, advertising men, reporters, and newscasters who proclaim the "Century of Progress" exposition as evidence of general ease and affluence. The polemic contains a series of anecdotes and case studies of deprived and exploited ethnic groups: "They're half sick from birth, so they grow up bad. Black kids, Wop kids, Swede kids, Hunkey, Litvak and Chinese kids — the skinny tough dirty knockabout kids that had to knock down a fence to get into the World's Fair playground."

No keen perception is required to recognize here the scene, tone, characters, and themes of the two important Chicago novels that soon followed from Algren's typewriter. In his later novels the author integrates such material more closely with the narrative, and he reserves the frontal attacks for such special works as *Chicago: City on the Make, Who Lost an American?* and the *Sea Diary*.

VII   *Assessment*

Somebody in Boots, then, is not the simply integrated and purely static "road story" which a succession of commentators have branded it. The events of the story are more than an "undifferentiated mass . . . movement without progress"[2] since the episodes are differentiated as components of a climactic, three-stage grouping in the wanderings of Cass McKay — movement which changes Cass from the raw, helpless neophyte of the road to the self-sufficient if still dispossessed wanderer which he is at the end of the story. Nor is the narrative told entirely in "the straight documentary style of the 1930's"[3] since few other major novelists of the decade, least of all the documentarists, utilize the highly imagistic and symbolic techniques through which Algren achieves considerable coherence.

Though armed with a depth and intensity of personal experience and direct observation, Algren avoids producing the Zola-esque "collective novel." Instead, Algren prefers to work in a literary milieu largely shunned by documentarists — the figurative, intense, probing studies of human sensibility struggling against hostile environment which Stephen Crane created in such remarkable stories as *Maggie, The Monster*, and *The Blue Hotel*.

In *Somebody in Boots,* Algren establishes this posture explicitly. He says of Cass McKay, "Not once in his young manhood was he to see the shadow of pain cross a human face without being touched to the heart. He was never to see a blow struck or a man beaten, in all his young manhood, but he would be sickened almost to fainting." The Cass McKays of the world are born with capacities for compassion and for perception of beauty which, however dulled or hardened by the grossness of their lives, might in another environment constitute a human being who is, if not a little lower than angels, certainly higher than jungle beasts.

VIII   A Walk on the Wild Side:
Transformed Values with Humor and Poetry

By the time the author of *Somebody in Boots* had become the first recipient of the National Book Award for *The Man with the Golden Arm* in 1949, most critics and reviewers had forgotten that Algren had begun as a chronicler of the South rather than as a Chicago novelist. *Somebody in Boots* had created so little stir that Algren was known almost exclusively as the "Division Street Dostoevsky" who had produced a neatly built Chicago prize-fighter novel called *Never Come Morning* and a shattering story about a Chicago dope addict, *The Man with the Golden Arm.*

When *A Walk on the Wild Side* was published in 1956, critics with few exceptions either had not read *Somebody in Boots* or did not remember it well enough to recognize the similarities between the two stories. Even fewer were aware that the new Algren novel had begun as a simple redaction of his first. Among dozens of reviewers at the time of publication, only Maxwell Geismar appeared to comprehend fully the implications of Algren's return to the Southern scene through a deliberate reworking of his unsuccessful first effort.[4] More than a year passed before George Bluestone assessed in perspective the relationships between *Somebody in Boots* and *A Walk on the Wild Side.* Though there is no evidence that Bluestone knew all the circumstances which led to the new work, he produced the first and in some ways still the best collation and comparison of the two novels. Noting that reviewers had tried to criticize *A Walk on the Wild Side* without recognizing its blood-ties to *Somebody in Boots,* he said: "To reviewers who had forgotten Algren's first novel, it [*A Walk on the Wild Side*] seemed a strange, even perverse, abandonment of the Chicago setting."[5]

According to Algren's own account, *Somebody in Boots* was almost forgotten by its author, reader, and publisher when Doubleday, the publisher of *The Man with the Golden Arm*, sought to capitalize in 1949 upon the success of that novel by reissuing *Somebody in Boots* in a paperback edition, one that was salable because the name of Algren then led the current best-seller lists. Algren, with a substantial advance from the publishers, returned to his youthful road story. His choice of title for his new version, *A Walk on the Wild Side*, he drew from the title of an unpublished essay he had written to refute McCarthyism during the Joe McCarthy era; but he no longer remembers where he got the idea for the title of that essay.[6]

Rereading the first few pages of his twenty-year-old story, he found the tone almost funny in its grimness. As he deleted passages, added new ones, and rewrote others, he saw that he was making of Cass McKay an altogether different character: "I began thinking of this clown who kept working into these situations; and so it became a kind of funny book. And a much better book — much more poetic than if I had started out to be poetic." Thus his discovery and development of a comic undertow in the grim *Somebody in Boots* transformed a mere editorial task into a story of which Algren has said, "It is the kind of novel that, so far as I know, has never been written before."[7]

The basic structure of the new novel is still that of the journey, and the opening scenes retain all the rudiments of the germinal tale. The fresh treatment keeps the already established "native son" motif as it traces the fortunes of a dispossessed American "tribe" of independent hunter-stock. In more specific terms, it is still the story of a "final descendant." The family unit — its heritage, its class, its composition — is fundamentally the same as that of the McKays; but the family has undergone a name change to Linkhorn, an older version of Lincoln, and it lacks one member who is significant in the earlier tale: the sister. No female survives in the Linkhorn clan, only Fitz the father, Byron the elder brother, and Dove — the youngest and last male member of the long-drawn, Scot-spawned "Fitzbrian's branch of the Linkhorn tribe."

Shorn to its essentials, the structure of the new tale emerges as materially different from that of the old. Embodying all the physical and mental characteristics of his tribe, with hair neither red nor yellow yet a blend of both, colorless brows, and shuffling walk, sixteen-year-old Dove Linkhorn is illiterate but innately canny. He appears at the ancient hotel on the edge of town, once the bawdy house where Fitz had met and conquered Dove's red-haired mother, but now the cafe owned and operated by Teresina Vidavarri,[8] the "Dolores del Rio" of Arroyo, Texas (population 955); and he requests her to read him the Sunday comics. He becomes Teresina's janitor and odd-jobber. Though Teresina is thirty-three and Dove only sixteen, the unlikely two are drawn together: she, by the emotional vacuum left from an early marriage to a perverted florist; he, by unconscious but fast-budding virility of staggering force.

After first seducing Teresina in her own bedroom and subsequently raping her beneath the clothesline in the back yard, Dove leaves her subdued and helpless, and catches the first freight train to Houston and New Orleans. Along the way, he meets and saves the life of the neophyte prostitute, Kitty Twist, who initiates him into the ways of the road, the soup-kitchen, the flop-house, casual sex, and general survival. Kitty is apprehended in a robbery she plans, but Dove escapes with forty-one dollars in his pocket.

In New Orleans during the depression, Dove finds rich soil for sowing the contributions unique to his heritage — blended Scots-and-Kentucky-hunter shrewdness and the virility brought down through generations of the wild-boy clan. With an instinct for spotting con operations and for capitalizing upon opportunities, Dove, eager to please, enters "the city that always seems to be rocking"; collects full pay for sitting at the top of a ship's smokestack he is supposed to paint; outwits a young prostitute who tries to lift his wallet; sells coffee pots and beauty-parlor certificates in door-to-door campaigns; works in a home-operated condom factory; and finds his highest talent in becoming an inexhaustible star performer as the daily deflowerer of ancient prostitutes who are advertised as virgins in Oliver Finnerty's prosperous peep-show.

As pimp and peep-show lecher, Dove scales all the heights attainable in his profession; but, in his compulsion to learn to read, he leaves Finnerty's house on Perdido Street to live for a time with another whore-house escapee, the ex-school-teacher Hallie, who tutors him to near literacy. But Hallie returns to her lover, the legless carnival strong man, Achilles Schmidt, who beats Dove permanently blind before being killed himself at the hands of the aroused barroom mob. Nearly helpless, Dove returns to Arroyo in search of the woman he had deserted there, Teresina Vidavarri.

No longer a true road story like *Somebody in Boots*, whose structure consists of excursion patterns and virtually ceaseless change of locale, *A Walk on the Wild Side* becomes the implicit journey of a young, illiterate Texan in search of himself and his place in the world. His rise to the top in a profession which society regards as the bottom is significant, since the transformation of conventional scales of value in this book is one of Algren's signal contributions to the development of the modern American novel.

That transformation begins with Algren's view of the Linkhorns as a fresh interpretation of the McKay family. Though the family heritage is basically the same for both families, Algren deepens and broadens the anthropological base by providing an explicit genealogy for the Linkhorns. For this contribution to his new story idea Algren credits his reading of W. J. Cash's *The Mind of the South* which had appeared in 1941. Through the incorporation of these new materials, the otherwise inexplicable facets of Dove Linkhorn's character are foreshadowed by his "wild boy" lineage that reaches back to the time when "the first rock had risen above the moving waters" and that provides a base for the Fitzbrians, a branch of those ancestral Linkhorns antedating the American Lincolns.

The history of the Linkhorns is a saga of the clan pitted incessantly against all higher authority: "Duke and baron, lord and laird, city merchant, church and state, landowners both great and small, had formed a united front for the good work. When a Linkhorn had finally taken bush parole, fleeing his Scottish bondage for the brave new world, word went on ahead: Watch for a wild boy of no particular clan, ready for anything, always armed. Prefers fighting to toil, drink to fighting, chasing women to booze or battle: may attempt all three concurrently."

Dove Linkhorn, sprung from the last family unit of such a lineage, emerges during the 1930's in Arroyo, Texas. His father's fathers had come to America as sharecroppers, but had hunted without cropping; they had boozed, fiddled, and sung the songs of Burns; they had disowned that presidential Linkhorn they held responsible for the Civil War; they had continued their ways through the tyranny of the mill owners who had succeeded the plantation owners; and they had wound up as "white trash" and "po' buckra" in the Rio Grande Valley where Fitz Linkhorn had married a red-haired prostitute, survived the failures of oil, cotton, and oranges, and was raising his family in the dust, earning his way by pumping cesspools with a hired rig.

The fully dramatized Linkhorn lineage produced in Fitz Linkhorn, not the simple and cruel father-figure of *Somebody in Boots*, but a true roisterer and wild-boy revivalist. Like Stub McKay,

Fitz is a man of unpredictable temper, a man against all popular dress and modern vices except liquor, a man consumed by the daily sense of having been cheated, a man whose only release is in "getting his back up." Unlike Stub, he does not react in the swift, instinctive, sometimes mindless manner of the jungle beast. Instead, he lashes out in travesties of the Almighty Word, with the general damnation of the town and the human race, and with the particular scarification of his eldest son, Byron, who serves as prod and foil for his father's regular Saturday night damnation-meetings on the steps of the courthouse.

Dove Linkhorn's childhood is different from Cass McKay's, then, in at least one important respect: Dove's faculties have not been tuned from infancy to the imminence of physical brutality and to the sense of death. Though Dove's home is a shack no more prepossessing than Cass's, he knows cruelty largely in terms of wild-boy roistering and verbal sparring rather than of beating and murder. His elder brother, Byron, is a "lunger," dying with lungs destroyed by the war; and he is hastening his death by smoking the potaguaya bush. He is a worthless cynic and scoffer, not like Bryan McKay, who was a brutalized brawler and decapitator of cats. To Fitz Linkhorn, the feeling of having been cheated is not focused upon a single "Damned Man" who must be thrown under a moving train; instead, Fitz, between swigs of corn liquor, washes out his hatred in public every Saturday night on the courthouse steps when he directs his wrath openly against all who do not believe in his own version of the New Jerusalem, against the "Papist Rapists" who are the real cheaters, and against all who voted for the Pope and Al Smith in 1928.

If Dove Linkhorn does not know the brutality which drove Cass McKay from home, neither does he know the kind of love which Nancy provided Cass. In fact, Dove "could not remember a time, a place nor a single person, house cat or hound dog that had sought his affection." His life is to be a search to replace the love of a mother whose long-lost presence he can evoke only when, in sleep, he sometimes "had a fleeting feeling that a woman with red-gold hair had just touched his hand and fled beyond a curtained door."

IX   A Born World Shaker

Dove, who is totally illiterate and socio-economically no better off than Cass McKay, possesses two attributes which make him a superstar in a depression world in which "the ladder of success had been inverted, the top was the bottom, and the bottom the top." These two forces are the profound drive for male sexual identity and the genetic accident which has concentrated in him, as a final descendant, all the natural and abandoned virility of generations of the wild-boy tribe. In one who must become "a walker in search of something to belong to in order to belong to himself," these latent forces lurk secretly, waiting only to be discovered. But, once discovered, they shoot Dove Linkhorn effortlessly, as a natural athlete, to championship class in virility — a sports arena never recognized by any chamber of commerce, better business bureau, or athletic association.

Algren controls with care the successive phases of his hero's self-discovery. The first intimation of Dove's sexual endowments occurs when, to the music of the jukebox in the old Hotel Davy Crockett, which is now Teresina's cafe, the sixteen-year-old Dove "invited all women in a grind so purified by lust that Teresina felt her own thighs start to part." From this moment, the seduction and the rape of Teresina are inevitable. After the seduction, Dove is exhilarated by his unsuspected prowess: "All I know for certain is I'm a born world-shaker."

When Algren helped prepare the dramatization of *A Walk on the Wild Side* that was presented at the Crystal Palace Theatre in St. Louis in the Spring of 1960, Dove's exultation at this point in his life and career is the subject of the following lyric, which Algren wrote for the musical:

Worldshaker

VERSE:

I can't read words and I can't write
But still I'm bound to state
That after what I done last night
I know I will be great.
I haven't figured out what kind of great I'll be
I'm not the common kind that's plain to see.

CHORUS:

I'm a born world shaker
And I'm bound to rise
'cause I got the power

That the women prize
I will climb the ladder
And it won't take long
I'm a born world shaker
and I'm bed cord strong
I'm a born world shaker
I'm a risin' star
And when I get goin'
I will travel far
Though there's some that take me
For a country clown
I'm a born world shaker
and I won't stay down
I've just got to pick me a line
There's money in hogs I been told
A tooth dentist, that would be fine
Or maybe I'll prospect for gold
As soon as I learn me a trade
And get these old feet in some shoes
I'm sure I can lead the parade
In any old town that I choose
Gonna learn my letters
All the way to Z
Though it's not decided
What I'm gonna be
I'm a born world shaker
And I can't go wrong
'Cause I'm bent on risin'
And I'm bed cord strong
I'm a real earth shaker
A big heart breaker
Just a born world shaker
That's me.

In the novel, Dove accepts future developments with no surprise. In New Orleans, he permits three one-dollar prostitutes to pull him into their doorways one after the other within a few minutes' time, and the only effect of his endeavors is to make him hungry. When selling coffee pots, he manages incidental coitus with a Negro woman in a rocking chair at the same time that he reaches beyond her head to repossess a coffee pot and suffers a mosquito attack on his bare buttocks. Finnerty, the master pimp, senses Dove's powers and snares him into the "studbum" trade by hiring him to "deflower" a "virgin" in his stable of prostitutes. Afterwards, with casual ease, with unflagging reserves of natural energy, and even with the flair of the ham actor, he performs several times daily, week after week, opposite the peepholes of Finnerty's enterprise.

A close counterpart of Dove's natural virility is his equally native shrewdness, a combination sometimes misunderstood by those who have not carefully examined Algren' purpose. To say, for instance, that "Mr. Algren has been kidding us about his hero, whose innocence turns out to be largely a pose; indeed, his instinctive cunning is so sharp that he can outsmart the wiliest whore or the shrewdest con man,"[9] is to ignore the care with which Algren has established for Dove a lineage which accounts for his innate slyness just as clearly as it does for his otherwise unaccountable virility. Dove is the last descendant of a canny Scots clan whose generations have made it their single purpose to occupy the fringes of society without contributing to it. In this important respect, the heritage of the Linkhorns is one long confidence game. To Dove Linkhorn, unconscious wiliness is the gift of a blood line so early conned out of its crops and other possessions that, for survival, its descendants are sensitized to the confidence game in all generations. Far from being a posed innocence, his cunning is more effective because it is unaffected.

Algren has called A Walk on the Wild Side "a very innocent book," and he apparently means that the story is without artificial trickery. Dove's naive shrewdness is intimately bound up with the prevailing innocence to which Algren refers. In the first place, Dove is basically a "clown"; but his early counterpart, Cass McKay, was just the opposite: plodding, slow of thought and perception, earnest to the point of grimness, painfully self-conscious, and generally humorless. But Algren in 1954 created in Dove a different endproduct of the wild-boy clan: a canny, colorful, and exuberant clown, a character of comic-strip vitality and visual appeal but of far greater than comic-strip complexity and significance — a character perfectly contrived to function as "an ironical parody of the American success story."[10]

After 1929, when the stock brokers "began jumping off rooftops with no greater consideration for those passing below than they'd had when their luck was running," and while "lawyers sued one another just to keep in practice," the occupational pariahs like Dove found their heyday. The pimps and ponces "of a sudden found themselves with more girls than beds to put them on," and Negro bellboys found that "white male guests either wanted a woman with a bottle or a bottle with a woman." This world, no longer the oyster of the "owners" and the traditionally affluent, had become a huckster's carnival where "everybody was out soliciting in one commodity or another." It was that rarest of all worlds, one in which the down-and-outers and the otherwise oppressed could rise to the top of the social and economic scale by exploiting what, in other worlds, had always been the lowest resources of the scale.

The clownishness and the "bumbling cunning"[11] of Dove Linkhorn are signal advantages in a novel devoted to presenting the "Horatio Alger Dream" in a new fashion. *A Walk on the Wild Side* is not, properly speaking, a travesty upon the Horatio Alger myth of "rising in the world." It is a travesty upon a world in which, since the lowest layer of society has become the top one, the force of the myth leads its practitioners to the lowest social level because that is where a special form of success lies. And for such a rise in such a society, what more appropriate character could be conceived than Dove Linkhorn, the "debauched Davy Crockett,"[12] the "youthful descendant of Voltaire's 'Candide',"[13] the "yellow-shoed stallion"?[14]

To serve Algren's purpose in this inverted society, Dove has to be a broader latter-day representative of the picaro than Cass McKay was born to be. "In his [Dove's] combination of naiveté and cunning and in his aptness for learning the worst things first,"[15] he is admirably fitted for that world. Not burdened by Cass's preoccupation with death, Dove is also "more innocent and more lucky";[16] and both qualities rise from his profound amorality, which prohibits in him all consciousness of sin, whatever his excesses. In this sense, he remains an eternal innocent. Among the dispossessed walkers on the wild side, therefore, he is that rare creature, the "loser" who cannot truly be victimized since his blend of naiveté and cunning is virtually impenetrable.

But to assume that his incapacity for sin renders him incapable of harboring a sense of guilt is misleading. It is too much to say that, through all his mistakes, he "not only remains essentially decent but grows in goodness."[17] He is sinless only because his special form of innocence prevents his perceiving the wrong in what civilized society calls "vice." Algren insists that any such creature must eventually suffer from his innocence since society will not long abide flagrant abuse of its laws. Furthermore, Dove is sensitive to his own wrong-doing whenever he fails those who have selflessly given to him. He has in this respect, in fact, what may be considered to be a conscience, and it is a source of his guilt.

X *Love and Guilt: The Reverence and the Yearning*

In *A Walk on the Wild Side,* as in each preceding novel, an important guilt motif appears. Reared in a womanless family and first
aware of his super-abundant sexuality in his association with
Teresina, the sixteen-year-old Dove is gripped simultaneously by
"that special reverence of men who have lived wholly apart from
women" and by a sexual yearning "deep as need can go." In his
callowness, unable to distinguish between the reverence and the
yearning, he conquers the emotionally starved older woman as easily
and as effectively as a grown man of mature sexual experience might
have done. Later, however, having left her subdued and broken, he
senses that he has violated that special reverence which he can have
for no other woman. During his first hours in New Orleans, he is
stabbed by this realization when his discovery of Teresina's
handkerchief gives him the "shadowy apprehension that he might
never hurt anyone except those who were dearest" and that, among
the "abundance of pangs," he will know one "that would never let
him go." Furthermore, as he stands gripped by this awareness, "the
light lay pasted like a second-hand shroud against a guilt-stained
wall."

A strong reliance upon symbolism appears in the complex of images surrounding Dove's sense of guilt, especially in regard to his
driving desire to achieve at least minimal literacy. The first thing he
says to Teresina Vidavarri, as he stands before her holding out the
Sunday comics, is "I don't know how letters make words."
Understanding that he is ashamed to ask anyone else, Teresina
"quotes" the comics to him. From that moment, the desire to read
becomes one of Dove's few obsessions — one always intimately con-
nected with Teresina and with his betrayal of her. The guilt of that
betrayal is conveyed repeatedly through the image of the little tin
soldier whose story Teresina had read aloud, thereby capturing
Dove's imagination forever.

To Dove, the story acquires a double symbolic force. First, the
one-legged soldier is incomplete physically, as Dove is in other ways:
there had been insufficient material to make either of them a
finished creature. Yet the little soldier "stood quite as well on his one
leg as others did on two," and Dove is certain that, "of the whole army, this was the one who would get to see most of the world, have
the greatest adventures and at last win the love that all the others
wanted too." But Dove finds the ending of the story unsatisfactory:

first, he refuses to believe that, after the adventuring is done, the little soldier must be thrown into the fire. Sensing that the story of the little tin soldier is potentially a parallel of his own life, Dove will not accept such an ending. Second, the image of the tin soldier recurs to Dove coincidentally during crucial moments of his career to serve as a constant reminder not only of his betrayal of both Teresina and himself, but also of the unsatisfactory end toward which his life could be moving. Upon Dove's first visit to the whorehouse where he is to fulfill his own bizarre career, the little tin soldier stares at him from the pages of Hallie Breedlove's book[18] which she had left upon the parlor sofa. From Hallie, the former schoolteacher, Dove at last learns to read; but he is then beaten until blind by her legless strongman lover, Schmidt.

When, in his blindness, Dove chooses to return to Teresina, his choice is neither ambiguous nor unforeshadowed: his guilt has driven him all the while toward that choice. Assuming it true that his "loss of ambition and his blindness together make up a form of salvation,"[19] where can he be expected to go, if not to that emotionally crippled but compassionate woman whom he had once awakened and then abandoned; to her of whom he had thought, in a moment of revelation, "My whole enduren life you were the only human to try to see could I live up to the alphabet"; to the one he had dreamed was searching for him, "wearing dark glasses and extending her arms to find her blind way"; to that compassionate being who had once asked herself, "Where was such a dunce to find another friend?"

XI *Room at the Top — and Bottom*

Another clearly symbolic episode occurs when Dove visits a "seacave" restaurant where many turtles have been beheaded in preparation for the soup kettle. Dove is fascinated by the struggles of one magnificent headless terrapin who is blindly driven to attain the very top of the pile of other headless turtles. Beside Dove is the head of the magnificent turtle, and "Dove and the Head watched together to see if the Body would make it." Believing, like all turtles, that "all things come to him who will but struggle," the turtle scales the top, where there is always room for one more, but it then topples to the bottom. Even then the real lesson does not occur to Dove: "there was also room for one more at the bottom."

The purpose of the decapitation symbol is different from that of a similar pattern in *Somebody in Boots* in which the succession of decapitations gives Cass a sense of the imminence of death. To Dove, the clown prince of wild-boy innocence, omnipresent Death-in-Life is unrecognizable and even, perhaps, irrelevant. The certainty of defeat and the chance of death cannot penetrate his innocence, however powerfully these forces charge the tone and atmosphere of Algren's tale itself. If Dove does not feel their imminence, the reader cannot miss it. And the special vitality of Dove's character lies in the abounding naiveté and the candid optimism which screen him from messages of defeat.

A *Walk on the Wild Side* is the only Algren novel so structured as to complete the action by bringing the protagonist back to the place and to the basic situation from which he had begun his journey or his entanglement. Furthermore, unlike *Somebody in Boots*, this novel achieves coherence through its structure rather than through a system of *leitmotifs*. "I was surprised when I went through it that I'd contrived better," said Algren, "because the plot dove-tailed and that was the first time I was able to do that."[20]

XII *Assessment by Critics*

The imagery and the ending sparked a re-evaluation of Algren's attitudes and purpose. The most common point of departure for the reassessments was Algren's own statement, printed on the back of the dust jacket of the first edition: "The book asks why lost people sometimes develop into greater human beings than those who have never been lost in their whole lives." With this authorial declaration as a base, critics and reviewers divided into several camps. One group was antagonistic toward a story which appeared to prove what a few critics had suspected all along — that Algren had finally disclosed himself as the radical champion for a class of people whom no sensible person could possibly accept on Algren's terms. The other critics, however, found the novel to be a confirmation of Algren's effectiveness as the compassionate chronicler of America's lost and dispossessed. Aside from these clearly defined groups of critics, others were enthusiastic in their praise of the novel as a new development in American fiction.

Another basis for these extremes of critical reaction is a set of passages in the novel itself — two or three statements which could be construed as the "ethic" of the story, one not unlike the lessons which Cass McKay had learned from his various excursions in *Somebody in Boots*. The first declaration is the ultimately rejected advice offered Dove by Gross, the manufacturer of garish contraceptives: "Look out for love, look out for trust, look out for *giving*. Look out for wine, look out for daisies and people who laugh readily. Be especially wary of friendship, Son, it can only lead to trouble." Another appears toward the end of the story when Dove is in jail with a seasoned rounder called Cross-Country Kline who tells him that rising in the present world is of little value "for that can't be done any longer except on the necks of others. And when you make it that way, all the satisfaction is taken out of it. . . . There's no trick in not going down the drain if you don't live in the sink." But more important is Dove's own recapitulation of what he has learned when he pauses in his jail cell after the death of Kline, to tell himself: "All I found was two kinds of people. Them that would rather live on the loser's side of the street with the other losers than to win off by theirselves; and them who want to be one of the winners even though the only way left for them to win was over them who have already been whipped." By the time Dove returns to Teresina, he has learned that, as one of the losers, he can hope for some measure of redemption only through denial of old Gross's ethic.

Algren's compassion for society's lost and dispossessed had been clear from his earliest works; but, with the appearance of *A Walk on the Wild Side,* the already hostile critics, and some heretofore undecided ones, accused him of "puerile sentimentality"[21] and of wild excess. One complained that "in supposing that human virtue flourishes best among degenerates, Novelist Algren has dressed his sense of compassion in the rags of vulgarity."[22] Other dissenters asserted that the novel was a "stitch-by-stitch examination of the ravelled seams of humanity,"[23] a representation of "a form of inverted sentimentalism of a very ancient order,"[24] or the juncture at which Algren began his pose, his stance — the platitudes and the sentimentality that have informed his work ever since.

The general reaction to the novel was favorable, however.[25] Most reviewers were willing to accept the premise that Algren had set himself "the extremely difficult literary task of showing how much basic human strength and worth can persist in lives which, outwardly, represent utter degradation."[26] In reviewing the critical reactions, Lawrence Lipton defended Algren's adherence to the "simple humanity" of St. Francis of Assisi and of Walt Whitman, and he invoked the injunction of G. K. Chesterton that the slum novelist "should present the slum dweller not as a poor man but simply as a *man*."[27] Such a view of man is "not sentimentality but a plain belief in the special humaneness of those who suffer."[28]

Some critics thought that Algren had found a literary mode which suited his talents as no other mode had ever done. "In a novel of immense vitality and imaginative exuberance,"[29] it became "his peculiar gift to portray with deep feeling the triumph of the defeated and the defeat of the triumphant."[30] Algren wrote "with enormous compassion, a feeling for the almost-beaten, the half-lost ones who cannot make their way in a world that gives its prizes to the conformists, to the already privileged."[31] To one, he seemed the "new headmaster of the Chicago school of realism."[32]

XIII *The Characters: A Covey of Queer Quail*

As the critical reaction indicates, Algren's success is partly the result of his having developed convincing and entertaining characters, even though they are a "covey of queer quail."[33] The queer quail include pimps and whores, sexual deviates, sadists, lushes, hoboes, "kleptoes," gamblers, con men, pickpockets, "cokies," and other assorted criminals and on-the-fringe people. But all are highly individualized, and none is ever dull. One of Algren's most remarkable achievements in *A Walk on the Wild Side* is his convincing, compassionate treatment of a group of characters who could, in less skillful hands, be little more than a gallery of freaks and sheer grotesques. Algren makes them believable and sometimes arouses sympathy in the reader by treating them as people with dreams and aspirations, however callous the world outside; with vitality, however debilitating the circumstances; with humor, however unfunny the situation; and with individuality, whatever the usual literary mold or stereotype.

The unforgettable legless man, Schmidt, who is Algren's own favorite character among his creations, is an example. Though a substantial literary tradition of partial or total amputees exists, Schmidt belongs to the family of neither Captain Ahab nor Porgy. Despite Schmidt's having displayed himself as a carnival freak, he as a man transcends his freakishness. Despite — or because of — his own virility, he is the only customer who turns away in disgust from Finnerty's peep show. Retaining all the original strength of his magnificent torso, yet doomed to move, however agilely, upon a wheeled platform, he bursts upon the reader as a complex and impressive human being rather than as a cripple. To laugh *at* Schmidt is unthinkable, though it is sometimes possible to laugh *with* him. Even more formidable than the strength of his arms is the strength of his pride. That he should die in defense of his wounded pride, and die in an almost Surrealistic scene of jungle-like barroom viciousness, is so fitting as to seem almost inevitable.

The man on the platform came directly out of Algren's own experience:

> The original legless man was named Freddy, and he lived in a boardinghouse in East St. Louis. He sold a colored water that passed for a perfume which he made in the bathtub. He hung around an East St. Louis tavern and was both admired and feared. He had lost his legs working as a fireman on the Michigan Central years before, and must have been well over six feet before the accident. Nobody, even when he was on his platform, thought of him as less. I believe he was the strongest man I've ever known. I don't mean just in physical terms. He had a strength of *person* that dominated every scene he occupied.
>
> People who suffer that violent an accident are often left mentally groggy. Freddy was clear as light, capable of tremendous rage, and yet a humorous and gentle man ordinarily.
>
> I have seen him many times since: wheeling down North Avenue in Chicago at three on a bitterly cold February morning. Again under an Arab's burnoose and without his platform, kneewalking through the *souk* at midday in Fez. I saw him coming downhill in the rain in a Welsh town called Llanelly; it was evening and there was a war on that was going to last forever, and I was hurrying to pick up a girl before the blackout curtains were pulled. The last time I happened on him was in the neighboring novelist's last book. That was the last time I'll see him. So long, Freddy.[34]

Freddy, who, as Railroad Shorty in "The Face in the Barroom Floor," appeared early in Algren's fiction, returned in the portrait of Schmidt; but he was not to reappear until the 1960 musical version of *A Walk on the Wild Side.* Algren disassociates himself completely from the 1962 movie version of his latest novel, which he never intends to see, even though Schmidt plays a substantial part in it. Called, like the novel, *A Walk on the Wild Side* and starring Laurence Harvey, Capuchine, Jane Fonda, Barbara Stanwyck, and Anne Baxter, it is still shown occasionally on television. Steven H. Scheuer is right in calling it "a muddled, botched-up drama based on Nelson Algren's hard-hitting novel about the sinful side of life in New Orleans."[35] When J. W. Corrington asked Algren about the film, he replied: "I haven't seen the movie. I also keep moving when I see a crowd gathering where somebody has been run over by a garbage truck."[36]

Algren, noting that he has since encountered his creation, the man on wheels, in the fiction of others, discusses the importance of

Schmidt in his own work: "The best thing I've done is *Walk*. And
the best thing in *Walk* is the legless man. And the legless man is the
most significant character I've done. I know this because he came
rolling along before *Neon Wilderness*, materialized in *Walk* — and
made the play, done at the Crystal Palace in St. Louis in the Spring
of 1960, memorable."

Algren wrote two lyrics for Schmidt to sing in that musical, "The
Room with the Low-Knobbed Door," which is included in the last
chapter of this book, and "The Man on Wheels," in which Schmidt
compares what he once was with what he has now become:

The Man on Wheels

The Birmin'ham Grizzly, that was me
Though the girls all called me their honey fed bear
When the show was finished the girls were there
There were kisses, confetti and wild applause
When the honey fed bear showed his terrible claws:
The Birmin'ham Grizzly, that was me
With the strength of seven and hard as a rock
Not a man on the circuit could break my lock
'Til the forty cold wheels and the freight train's roar
Left me there in the room with the low-knobbed door.
One off at the hip, one off at the knee.
The Birmin'ham Grizzly, that was me.
Now I see the two leggers hurrying by
To home, to love and to rest
As none take my envy, so none keep my love
The love that's locked in my chest.
The iron years, like the iron wheels
Have rolled over me but I won't cry out.
If death finds my step I'll just wheel about
He'll work up a sweat and he'll draw short breath
When I put my head lock on Mr. Death.
The Birmin'ham Grizzly, that was me
But a man on wheels is a kind of a clown
He can tell when a two legger's smiling him down
Yet it's all in the game and it's all in a day
Take the bitter along with the sweet I say
And I'll give any man the same square play
The Santa Fe wheels gave me.

In depicting "the girls," Algren, with a freshness and vividness
unequaled in similar fiction,[37] avoids the centuries-old stereotype of

the "good-hearted whore." The house girls on old Perdido Street are no more the tragi-comic whores of the seventeenth- and eighteenth-century stage than they are the bland, generous girls of John Steinbeck's *Cannery Row*. To Algren, the "oldest profession" is a subject neither for righteous sermonizing nor for a romantic cliché; a business like any other, it is distinguished by its long history as a profession and by its location at the margin of the law. Otherwise, pimps and whores are bosses and workers; and the workers "are people, good, bad, and indifferent, like any other women. If they perform a good deed or an unselfish act their motives are as mixed as those of any wife or sweetheart — or any businessman on the make for a buck."[38] In settling for the unvarnished view of a profession so long distorted by other considerations, Algren has studied his characters as people who have adopted a time- and self-consuming business, whatever the moral aspects of the business, and whatever the idiosyncracies of the individuals.

However picturesque as a character, Oliver Finnerty, the pimp who "claimed to be five foot but had to be wearing his cowboy boots to make good the boast" and who was "proprietor of six peepholes on the second floor of Spider-Boy Court," was first of all dedicated to the classic principles of professional pandering and was eminently successful in the business. In fact, he was highly progressive in the profession; and, like any other competitive businessman, he was proud of his ingenuity and efficiency, especially of being among the first panders in the South to see the potential in the "bug trade" and to transport his women by airplane. As a result, his five women were vain in the intra-professional knowledge that they were "swung" by Finnerty. They worked for a good company and were generally grateful to be kept in line by Finnerty's impersonal thwacks on the nape of the neck where marks would not give them excuse for missing work. Moreover, all were thorough converts to a professional code in which the only true disgrace was "honest labor."

In the lyrics for the musical version, however, the girls, growing older in a profession in which age is even a greater consideration than in most, long for retirement and for a change of scenery as they sing their regret:

This Life We've Led

This life we've led has left us strange
And now it's late for us to change
Our luck runs out, our dreams grow old

In rooms where love is bought and sold.
This life we've led, we would not choose
But some must win and some must lose.
The dancers grind, the music blares
You break your heart and no one cares.
I want to go where green things grow
And find some peace before the end
And when I leave I will not grieve
Except for you, my poor, lost friend.
If there's a God who sees our pain
Perhaps he'll say, "well, try again."
I'll think of you in years ahead
But I'll be glad when I forget
This life we've led.

XIV   Style: A Virtuosity Performance

Algren's colorful, unorthodox prose style elicited even more
critical comment after the appearance of A Walk on the Wild Side
than it had in the past. Algren often speaks of his fiction as poetry,
and his style is, in at least the broadest sense, poetic. Yet, like Whitman, he writes of matters which have not been historically
acceptable as poetic; and, in his novels, he has been particularly
vulnerable to the charge that his style is "blurred" because it alter-
nates between hard-cast realistic prose and passages of lyricism. In
the ribald, Rabelaisian tone of A Walk on the Wild Side, however,
this alternation creates precisely the effect which the subject matter
demands.

Algren disclaims deliberate poetizing in this book, however, and
the lyric tone is in general more closely integrated with the prose and
less obtrusive than in the Chicago novels. For the most part, he relies
upon snatches of popular jukebox tunes and upon an occasional short
near-metrical passage that warrant the comment that he "frames his
materials in back-country balladry and earthy lyricism."[39]
Otherwise, he concentrates upon capturing the true music of dialect
and upon exercising his keen ear for prose rhythms in which the
natural repetition and the metric rise and fall of colloquial speech
predominate. When asked the purpose of the rhyme and rhythm of
certain passages in A Walk on the Wild Side recently, Algren
replied, however, that "I guess I'd better rewrite the book again."

But the true stylistic unorthodoxies appear in his syntax and imagery far more than in his propensity for borderline versifying. From
the beginning of his career, he has experimented with unconven-

tional techniques of punctuation to achieve special effects. By the time he was writing the Chicago novels, he had wrought the techniques into a distinctive stylistic manner that was unlike that of any other novelist. His basic technique is to bind together a succession of individual fragments through the syntax which normally controls a long single sentence. Sometimes he varies this effect by using a short, uncomplicated run-on sentence. By the time he wrote *A Walk on the Wild Side*, he had fine-tuned this technique, frequently omitting "spare parts,"[40] until it was capable of conveying subtle nuance and astonishing variety of effect.

The result is that, during moments of high emotional pitch, his sentences and paragraphs break into an almost limitless variety of specially designed sentence fragments — all controlled by their being part of an otherwise conventional set of antitheses, subordinates, or coordinates. The effect is that of high rhythmic flexibility that has unusual prose control of pause and acceleration and that ranges from crackling staccato through crescendo. It is common, then, to find such syntactical virtuosities as the following shattered pattern of adverbial clauses, coordinate clauses, appositives, and implicit imperatives — one describing a moment during Dove's night in a flophouse:

Under wire on either side other dime-a-nighties slept out their ten-cent dreams. Till the hundred harps of morning struck on strings of silvered light.

And down the long unshaded street a vendor of colored ices beat a rainbow of tin bells. A bell for every flavor as he tinkle-tinkled past. Every flavor made of water sold to tunes made out of tin.

Come bummies, come beggars, two pennies per tune.

This kind of syntactical variety is Algren's rhetorical base, and he stretches its potential to the limit. It can be direct and literal, or it can be figurative and rhapsodic, but it is seldom dull or pedestrian.

In *A Walk on the Wild Side*, Algren utilized his rhetoric to develop devices of imagery with which he had long practiced. Like Stephen Crane's, his color-imagery had always been startling. In the Chicago novels, for instance, he had developed almost to the point of mannerism the device of coupling figurative noun-modifiers with the participle *colored*. The effects of the practice were impressive but startling since the modifiers were generally not words with a true or specific color designation. In the Chicago novels a man's cap is almost habitually described as "pavement colored." Though to most readers the image is gray, the modifier compound offers a range or choice of hue with the added dimensions of texture and suggestive tone. Few such compounds in the Chicago novels, however, are such broad use of the device as is the description of evening as "slander-colored" in *A Walk on the Wild Side*. Further, by the time Algren was reworking *Somebody in Boots*, he had begun to use extensively such highly specialized figures as forms of inverted personification: "It was fantasy that had pursued them, every one, all their lives; they had not pursued it."

But in *A Walk on the Wild Side*, as in Algren's previous novels, the impressive verbal mortar which binds the other stylistic properties is still the concreteness and specificity of detail; the accurate terminology of road, gutter, bar, and brothel; the keen and comprehensive ear for dialect; the eye for significant idiosyncracies of dress and behavior; the quick grasp of obsessive quirks of thought — the ring of authority. With the true novelist's ability to record and recall every detail which his senses register — especially all that he hears — Algren is able to re-create the little-known twilight world of the pander and the prostitute with a convincingness rarely matched in fiction. A "curious blend of poet and reporter, a kind of prose Walt Whitman,"[41] he combines the sensitivity and emotion of the poet with the factual sense of the good journalist. One reads such writers as Algren not simply for the vigor and excitement, though *A Walk on the Wild Side* abounds in these, but also because of the unavoidable impression that one is learning something valuable from a writer who knows his material.

Stylistically, *A Walk on the Wild Side* is a virtuoso performance, sometimes almost too rich, but never static; and the style justifies such comments as "his sentences are more direct and sparkling, his selectivity more keen and economical, and his symbolism richer and at the same time more complex"[42] than in his previous work. Altogether, this novel is the best example of "the wild and wonderful bird cage world of words that is Mr. Algren's special province."[43]

All these elements — the ethic, the characterization, the style — are fused and raised to a higher caliber by the maturing of Algren's sense of comedy, the ribald, grotesque, near-Surrealistic humor which informs all of *A Walk on the Wild Side*. In a recent critic's words, we have "the book to read and re-read and to enjoy and to learn from with every reading."[44] Algren's whole career had tuned him, as it were, to write this book. It is his own favorite and, he believes, his best.

CHAPTER 4

The Ultimate Underdogs: Never Come Morning

W ITH the appearance of *Never Come Morning* in 1942, Algren acquired the tenacious sobriquet of "poet of the Chicago slums." Since 1936 he had lived in or near Chicago; there he had married and divorced his first wife, collected folklore for the Illinois Works Progress Administration Writers' Project, worked on the Venereal Disease Control Program of the Chicago Board of Health, and written widely upon matters close at hand with enough success that "A Bottle of Milk for Mother" had been selected as an O. Henry Memorial Prize Story and had set the scene and tone for the two "Chicago novels" which followed it. The appearance of *The Man with the Golden Arm* and *Chicago: City on the Make* within the next nine years reinforced Malcolm Cowley's slum-poet label[1] and bound Algren permanently to Chicago.

To Algren, however, such labels are spurious and misleading. Admitting that he always seems to return to Chicago, he rejects tendencies to limit the significance of his literary work to localized geographic boundaries. Chicago and New Orleans, he says, are meaningful only because they are true microcosms; for he insists that what he writes is equally true of life in any big American city during the eras of which he writes.[2] The terms "Chicago novels" and "Southern novels" are useful, therefore, only to distinguish the two major locales of Algren's fiction; and the use of such terminology should not imply that the novels are essentially municipal studies or local color works.

With *Never Come Morning,* Algren assumed his place among other Chicago novelists who had begun writing during the depression years. Like Richard Wright, he spoke on behalf of those who could not speak for themselves. Wright's specific mission, in such works as *Native Son* and *Black Boy,* was to open "a wedge for the inarticulate of the world, both black and white."[3] Aside from the uniqueness of the Negro problem in America, however, the concerns of Algren were much like those of Wright. The two writers, who met at the Chicago John Reed Club in 1936 and who also served with the Chicago Works Progress Administration Writers' Project, recorded the fears and aspirations of discrete groups of ethnic inarticulates in the big city; and, in the process, they created stories of living nightmare.

Both of Algren's Chicago novels dissect the lives of Poles trapped and doomed by the intricate cultural and economic machinery of the vast city. The earlier book, *Never Come Morning* (1942), is a study of first and second generation urbanized Polish people, a group conscious of its identity as Poles; therefore, unlike the American-thinking Irish of James Farrell's stories, these Poles are only half Americanized. In this respect, Algren's Poles are closer literary kin to the exploited Lithuanians of Upton Sinclair's *The Jungle*. In exploring the gaps between Old-World and New-World values, Algren transcends other members of the Chicago school of Realism in his willingness to offset bleakness with lyricism, hopelessness with aspiration, and toughness with compassion.

I   Never Come Morning:
Hoodlumhood in Chicago's Little Poland

Bruno "Lefty" Bicek is the son of an immigrant Pole who, like the father in "How the Devil Came Down Division Street," played a piano-accordion in Division Street bars. At his death, he leaves an immigrant-Polish widow who has borne four sons; and of them only Bruno survives more than ten years. Now seventeen, endowed with "all the health that had been denied her other children," Bruno lives idly with his hypochondriac and bedridden mother in the family shop, Bicek's Imperial Milk Depot and Half-Price Day-Old Bakery. Like others of his generation, he is a grievance to relief workers and a bitter disappointment to his mother because at fourteen he spent two nights in jail without showing any remorse. His mother is consumed by bitterness: "If they had stayed in the Old World, she felt, her son would have been a good son." Her Old-World faith shattered, she has "taken no pleasure in him" since the jail episode.

At the beginning of the novel, Bruno is upon the threshold of a crucial two-day passage "from dependence to independence. From boyhood to manhood. From vandalism to hoodlumhood." He is "divided in his ambitions between being a big-league hurler and becoming a contender for the heavyweight championship of the world." Over looked by big-league scouts and under orders from the neighborhood crime boss, Bonifacy "the barber" Konstantine, Bruno becomes a gang leader by stealing a slot machine and by reorganizing the forty-odd "Warriors" under a new name, the "Baldheads." The membership badge is an army haircut purchased exclusively from "the barber." Now under the aegis of Bonifacy and Casey Benkowski, Bruno knows he must settle for a career as a boxer.

In gang idiom, Bruno's "jump" is Steffi Rostenkowski. Though Bruno and Steffi were "born two months apart on the same street," only now have they accepted each other in a yet unconsummated love affair. After the slot-machine theft, while Steffi's widowed mother is busy running her poolroom below, Bruno goes upstairs to Steffi's bedroom and seduces her; and he does not remember the charge of his gang friend Finger Idzikowski: "Let us know when you do. Then we c'n all score."

Next evening at a crap game in the Warriors' clubhouse under the sidewalk, Bruno asserts his new leadership by making this official announcement: "The Twenny-six Ward Warriors Social 'n Athletic Club is hereby dissolved by order of me 'n the barber, 'n this shed is getting boarded up, 'n the fellas who still want a place to shoot craps 'n bring dames 'n belong to a baseball team with uniforms . . . better show up tomorrow mornin' in front of Bonifacy's. All we have t' do is clean up his back room 'n take the Haircut Pledge." As he falls asleep on the plank floor of the disbanded clubhouse, Bruno congratulates himself upon his new stature in hoodlumdom: "I'm a executive you. I take the credit. Some day I'll leave the barber out too."

Within a week, however, he learns that he is only a flunkey in the hands of schemers and vicemongers like the barber and his henchmen. After an evening with Steffi at the Riverview Amusement Park, Bruno buys a bottle of cheap liquor and takes her to the rusty bedsprings in the boarded-up clubhouse. There, though he has sworn to himself that no other man will touch Steffi, he is psychologically paralyzed when Fireball threatens him, first with the knife which Bruno has always feared, then with the knowledge that he has been framed into stealing a syndicate shot machine. Threatening to squeal to the syndicate, Fireball takes control of the girl and the gang.

While Bruno roams numbly on the street, a long line forms to rape Steffi in the shack below. Helpless but infuriated, Bruno attacks a Greek outsider who muscles into the line. With a neck-breaking kick on the point of the Greek's jaw, he murders the interloper, whereupon the line dissolves into the shadows and the gang rape is over. Fireball and Catfoot then take the girl to the barber who places her under the "protection" of Mama Tomek. With respectability destroyed, Steffi becomes a prostitute in Mama Tomek's whorehouse. Her helplessness and passivity have rare appeal for the barber; so she serves also as his mistress, sleeping in his room above the Broken Knuckle Bar.

Three months after the rape of Steffi and the murder of the Greek, Bruno is hauled into Police Captain "One-Eye" Tenczara's query room where he is charged with shooting a drunk in an alley hallway. Though Casey Benkowski is guilty, Bruno refuses to reveal that information. He outlasts solitary confinement, a visit to the psychiatrist, a line-up, a beating, and a succession of nerve-twisting interrogations by the wily Tenczara who uncannily suspects Bruno of killing the Greek. Convicted of the crime he did not commit, Bruno spends six months in the House of Correction and emerges to start his boxing career all over again. He hopes to be as great as his idol, the incomparable ex-champion Tiger Pultoric.

Meanwhile, however, Bruno works as pimp and bouncer at Mama Tomek's where Steffi has been for nearly a year both a prostitute and the barber's mistress. Bruno is unable to express his remorse to Steffi, so they rarely talk; but they are keenly aware of each other. When the barber learns that Steffi has helped Bruno cheat him by flashing signals from behind his chair during a poker game, he beats her viciously; and, threatening to tell Tenczara that Bruno murdered the Greek, he makes her promise to avoid Bruno.

Infuriated because Finger, Casey, and Bruno have independently arranged a bout, the barber insists upon one breach of his compact with Steffi: she is to entice Bruno into their room and get him drunk on the night before the fight. She agrees rather than condemn Bruno. When Bruno appears he refuses to drink, expresses his remorse for abandoning her, and persuades her to agree to marry him after the fight when he will have sufficient money for them to escape the life they must now lead. But, before they can leave the room, they are attacked by Fireball, Catfoot, and Bruno's hero (the ex-champion Tiger Pultoric) who have been sent by the barber to make sure that Steffi succeeds in incapacitating Bruno. Though Bruno smashes his knuckles, he beats them all; and he takes from Fireball the long knife which has been the symbol of Bruno's fear. As Bruno leaves, Steffi feels for the first time that everything is "going to be all right after all."

The next night Bruno knocks out Honeyboy Tucker in the ninth round and achieves his lifelong dream: he is now a contender for the heavyweight championship of the world. Even more important, he will now have the money and power to protect Steffi. But he has underestimated the barber. While Bruno soaks a broken hand in the dressing room, One-Eye Tenczara walks in. "Got you for the Greek Left-hander," he says. Bruno's only answer is, "I knew I'd never get t' be twenty-one anyhow."

II *Old World vs. Young America*

Directly out of Chicago's "Little Poland" has come the story of Bruno Bicek's entanglement with social and economic forces which he can neither comprehend nor control. Like the other "Baldheads," he has been born into a web of adverse circumstance already woven, at least in part, by the same forces which have defeated his immigrant parents. And, though his values are those of Young America, they are not an effective substitute, he is to find, for the Old-World ones with which his generation is constantly at odds.

In *Never Come Morning*, the old-century old-people are forever strangers in the new land. Those who are honest and simple work their lives away playing accordions in bars, like Bruno's father; they suffer dumbly in small shops, like Bruno's mother; or they hold fast to enterprises like the poolroom perpetuated by Steffi's widowed mother. But they are people of principle. Bruno's mother has "the peasant faith in work as a cure-all." She cannot understand why her own son, at fourteen, could think "nothing of being two days in jail." She longs for the Old-World custom of putting troublesome boys in the army, for "the army made them good." With suspicion of all that is unfamiliar in the New World, she counters Bruno's explanation that prizefighting is a business with the query, "Is *crooked* business?"

But other older immigrants, who assume that everything is crooked, live by complete abandonment of all principle. Such are the small-time, non-syndicate, neighborhood vice-lords (like the half-crippled barber) who live by preying upon the lost women and upon the young among their own people. Like Stub McKay of *Somebody in Boots*, who "felt that he had been cheated with every breath he had ever drawn; but he did not know why or by whom," the barber lives perpetually under the conviction that "they were always trying to cheat him in this country." But, unlike Stub McKay, the barber knows precisely who his cheaters are: they are the players — even the imaginary ones — in the card game he runs, the whores who work for him at Mama Tomek's, the stupid and self-seeking minions like Casey Benkowski, all the young punks and budding hoods among the Warriors-Baldheads. The barber wins by cheating everybody else first, and there is not one over whom he does not hold some deadly threat. As each young punk like Bruno Bicek ripens into hoodlumhood, the barber forces the already trapped ones to trap the neophyte through some act which brings him into the fold. Like an owl whirling its head to see everywhere, and "too old to understand any need that was not the need for money," the barber lives every moment with his brain and his eyes alert to outcheat all the cheaters in a country where Old-World principles are only cheater's bait.

To the simple and honest among the immigrant generation, then, the American Dream has flickered and expired; and they are bitter but passive. To others, the Chicago of *Never Come Morning* still represents the Land of Opportunity; it is always potentially a Horatio Alger world where Success might wait on any pavement corner. An intermediary between the old generation and the new, the barber pursues Success in card cheating and in manipulation of the gullible. A monster of intrigue, he knows that in the offspring of his own generation lurks a rich vein of exploitable American Dream: the newspaper-headline mirage of success as a professional baseball player or the tabloid vision of fame as a champion prizefighter.

To the young Poles of the Damen-and-Division-Street neighborhoods, Success awaits only their emergence into the bargaining power of hoodlumhood. "Starved, warped, ignorant little egoisms,"[4] they belong neither to the old land nor to the new; they occupy a shadowed borderland between, one newly spawned of the old but not yet chartered to the new. Under stress, they lapse into the old tongue; and their very names bespeak their hybrid culture — American nicknames coupled with Polish surnames: "Lefty" Bicek, "Fireball" Kodadek, "Catfoot" Nowogrodsky, "Finger" Idzikowski. And, in the clear-cut ethnic ecology of the neighborhoods, all enemies or opponents are distinguished by Old-World nationality: Mex, Greek, Litvak, Wallio.

To the women of the inner cities, severing Old-World ties is even more difficult. As repositories of the domestic mores and folkways of the old country, the older women, like the widows Bicek and Rostenkowski, exist precariously on whatever their husbands left them; and they shake their heads at the spectacle of their young. The middle-aged succumb to whoredom. Among those on the verge of womanhood, Steffi is a fair example: "one of those women of the very poor who feign helplessness to camouflage indolence." Like her male counterparts, she quickly learns to distrust the rewards for honest endeavor; therefore, "her indolence was that of one who fears that, if she fulfills one duty well and swiftly, she will be called upon immediately for a less pleasant one. So the girl had made it her habit to do all things slowly and half-heartedly where they did not immediately concern her own pleasure." With such attitudes, young women like Steffi have narrow choices: to accept the best man available among the neighborhood gangs, or to accept anybody and become a prostitute. Except for Algren's caricature of the suspicious, moralistic type of relief worker, these are the only women in *Never Come Morning*.

Most of the secondary characters are limited in thought and action, and the capsulized *vita* of Casey Benkowski is typical. Having dutifully taken "a dive" in the prizefight scene with which the novel begins, Casey (for Casimer) enters through the alley door of Bonifacy's barber shop and stands looking at the sordid back room: "He had seen this room a thousand days of his life and wished he had seen it not once. In it he had become a bicycle thief when he was ten, a pimp when he was fourteen, and a preliminary boy at sixteen. Now, at twenty-nine, he had come, with the alley light behind him, to learn what the room wished him next to become." It is significant that, at seventeen, Bruno Bicek's life has been roughly the counterpart of Casey's — a jailbird at fourteen and already a victor in two important preliminary bouts, he is soon to become a pimp, a pawn of the same barber in the same room.

III   *Bruno's Fatal Flaw*

Unlike Casey and the others, Bruno "Lefty" Bicek has high promise as a prizefighter; and this potential is dangerous since it makes him the only threat to the barber's well-oiled machine. Bruno's mortal flaw as a Division-Street tribesman, however, is the touch of "frail humanity"[5] which sets him apart from his peers and renders him vulnerable to a jungle-like system based upon mutual exploitation and mindless courage. Despite his superb strength and coordination, Bruno is innately "soft" by the standards of the well-defined pecking order which he aspires to dominate; for he is incapable in decisive moments of defending his position against the inferior but ruthless members of the urban tribe: "Lefty Biceps wasn't really tough, everyone knew that." Until far too late, therefore, the homicidal moron called Fireball Kodadek, whose breath smells of "sen-sen mixed with canned heat," manipulates Bruno at will.

Worse yet, Bruno is "thin-skinned." In view of the hoodlum code by which he must live, he is far too sensitive. Compared with those among whom his lot is cast, he is almost a visionary who has the fatal propensity for endless daydreams and internal dialogue which not only heighten the contrast between what is and what ought to be but which also obscure the differences between vision and reality. In a world in which human empathy or sympathy is a booby trap, he tries to forsake the gang code in order to reserve his sweetheart for himself alone and to defend her against violation. Knowing that what belongs to him belongs also to the gang, "he decided fiercely that no one else was going to sleep with her ever; as though others, unseen, were already challenging his exclusive right to any girl."

He feels vaguely that he has wronged Steffi by seducing her. Even after demanding such a small demonstration of faith as forcing her to give him a dollar from her mother's cash register, his impulse is to "make it all up to her." His fatal weakness is an uncultivated but undeniable sub-sense of decency and fairness which prevents his total commitment to an inflexible code requiring the negation of these qualities.

Beyond his knowledge and despite his effort to the contrary, Bruno is by nature a "loner" and an outsider: "in the heart of the city . . . he walked alone." To the rest of his companions the mystique of the tribe is ingrained; its arcane limitations and demands are ineffable and as much a part of their thinking as the Polish-American street argot in which they speak. Their prime aspirations are to scheme, slash, and bludgeon their way as high as possible in the familiar pecking order. Chief among Bruno's fellow climbers, Fireball Kodadek "is like a cretin;"[6] a slasher with a spring-blade, a six-foot-four-inch failure as a pitcher, and "lean as tuberculosis," he schemes to take over the barber's women, even as he wastes away on a steady diet of whisky, though "the more he drank the thinner he got, the soberer he became, and the more desperate in his hopes and jealousies." Catfoot Nowogrodski, a lecherous satellite of Fireball, is a sneak, a lurker in shadows. Bibleback is a weakling who takes refuge in spurious righteousness and self-denial but invokes the sop of penance in order to take part in the rape — and he later tells the police about Bruno. Finger Idzikowski is a small-time "hex-man" and boxing trainer, and Casey Benkowski is a worn-out prizefighter-turned-manager; both aspire beyond the barber's sphere by tying their hopes to Bruno's talent, only to find that their comet is a falling star.

IV *Theme and Tone: Empathy and Seriousness*

Algren used these lines from Whitman as an epigraph for the novel:

> I feel I am of them —
> I belong to those convicts and prostitutes myself —
> And henceforth I will not deny them —
> For how can I deny myself?

This shift to Whitman from the Marxist quotations prefacing the Chicago sections of *Somebody in Boots* suggests that Algren had begun to modify the political force of his city fiction in order to achieve a broader theme. However, the prevailing tone of *Never Come Morning* is an extension of the abiding seriousness of *Somebody in Boots*, for Algren had not yet cultivated the comic genius which reached its height in *A Walk on the Wild Side*. Yet he demonstrated his growing maturity as an artist by interweaving in a story potentially grimmer than *Somebody in Boots* the coarse and juvenile wit of the young gangsters, the corrosive comedy of Tenczara's quips, and the pathetic pantomime of Bruno's "detation waltz."

Because the sharper focus of his scene and the subtler and more complex interaction of his characters helped dispel the suffused grimness of the earlier tone, the result is something more nearly akin to a mood poem, one especially appropriate to the sense of imminent death which he also carried over from *Somebody in Boots*. The death sense, culminating with Bruno's terminal admission, "I knew I'd never get t' be twenty-one anyhow," permeates all Bruno's daydreams and aspirations. It lurks, particularly, in the system of motifs and symbols which dominates the mutually destructive love affair of Bruno and Steffi.

V *Love and Guilt*

In *Never Come Morning*, as in all of Algren's novels, love is at the same time a necessity, a luxury, and an agent of nemesis; and love is intimately bound up with a guilt motif and with a yearning for redemption. The love affair of Bruno and Steffi, however, is Algren's lone excursion into adolescent love with its special esthetic problems of inexperience combined with callowness and lack of perspective. The world of Bruno and Steffi permits no romantic love, for the seventeen-year-old Polish lovers in the Chicago slums are too warped and stunted for a Romeo-Juliet affair or even for the *West Side Story* variation of it.

To Bruno, "life was a series of lusts: for tobacco so good he could eat it like meat; for meat, for coffee, for bread, for sleep, for whisky, for women, for dice games and ball games and personal triumphs in public places." Yet, from a childhood fear of cold and hunger, "he retained a wistful longing for the warmth and security of the womb"; and he thinks of himself, not figuratively[7] but literally, as a wolf of the streets and the alleys, "a hunter in a barren place." Beset eternally by insatiable hungers, he is "too hungry for the arid place he'd been born in. For lights, music, the women of the *gospodas*."[8] Above all, he lusts for something, anything, which he does not have to share with others. " 'I been hungry all my life, all the time,' he told himself, 'I never get my teeth into anythin' all my own.' " Incapable of making distinctions among love, lust, and the sheer urge for possession, but yearning for warmth and security, Bruno hovers in an air of twilight emotion. He senses the lasting worth of unselfish love, but he is unable to see women as anything but a utility.

His vision of what love ought to be, however, is the only aspiration which can carry him beyond his vainglorious search for newsreel success as a prizefighter. Near the end, but far too late, he turns to the hope of selfless married love with Steffi as the only means of transforming the "crooked business" of boxing into something more substantial than glorified hoodlumhood. Haunted from the beginning by the vision of redeeming love, he cannot resist his impulses to perform pathetic small acts of gallantry at which the rest of the tribe sneer. "What would Casey think of a president and treasurer who was lovesick?" In his world, then, he is fully aware that his vision is unrealizable — that he and Steffi are destined to be cheated of the real thing. At best, for them, love is "the only source of warmth in the lives of the hopeless";[9] and Bruno tallies this ultimate deprivation along with all the others which, cumulatively, fill him with cold rage.

Bruno's abandonment of Steffi to the gang rape, the scene "that most people will remember,"[10] has sources, therefore, that are far deeper ones than his fear of Kodadek's knife; and they are even deeper than mere compliance with gang-ethic. Beyond the fact that "to be regular was all he had ever been schooled to accomplish," Bruno has become bitterly aware that he lives in a world in which all trust is a sham, a world in conspiracy to take all good things from him. The hours preceding the rape scene thoroughly prepare Bruno to believe that even love is a hoax and not worth defending. His seduction of Steffi has been less a seduction than a half-hearted ritual, one robbed of meaning because each performs mechanically; Bruno complies with the expectations of the gang; and Steffi succumbs to the inevitable. Afterward, he is wracked by uncertainties. "If a girl was really a good girl," he thinks, "she ought to have sense not to bother with a Polack who had barely finished the eighth grade."

And, on the crucial evening when he takes her to the amusement park because he feels he owes her the pleasure, he perceives in all the glitter and ballyhoo a symptom of the intolerable falseness of his own barren life. As he pitches balls to win his girl a doll, he is consumed by a daydream in which he views himself as a big-league pitcher; then, enraged by the gulf between the ideal and the actual, he mutilates Steffi's doll because it is a "stuffed thing." At the top of a roller-coaster, he looks down upon the crowds and lights; and he thinks that "The park's a fake . . . Ever'thin's a fake." And, while Steffi presses herself hard against him in fear of the heights, he suspects that she, too, must be part of the universal fakery: "Wouldn't she be pressing just as hard against Catfoot if he bought the tickets?"

But Bruno is equally aware that his own inadequacies are as much to blame as Steffi's. In a closed society where "ever'-thin's crooked," the concept of trust is warped; therefore, the bond of interdependence which is Bruno's and Steffi's single bulwark against a perfidious world is unattainable because Bruno is unsure of his own steadfastness. He questions Steffi's worth on the basis that he himself is unworthy. As he capsulizes the ethic of suspicion, "You couldn't trust the ones with brains, because they had them, and you couldn't trust the ones without, because they didn't," he is deeply irritated with Steffi because "she had put trust in him, who had no trust in himself." That which should be the strength and comfort of their interdependence becomes, instead, the prime barrier to it. Since every evidence of her trust is an offense against his lack of faith in himself, he resents her reiterated declarations of belief; and, when he demands, "Don't you trust me?," his words are the perverse outcry of one who knows what he ought to give but cannot. At the moment when he abandons her to the gang, then, he can think "the hell with her, the hell with Catfoot, the hell with everything." In agreeing to go into the clubhouse with Bruno, Steffi had already implicitly abandoned herself with the thought, "I got nothin', so I got nothin' to lose."

Bruno's surrender of Steffi to the gang is not, therefore, merely the result of weak moral fiber nor even of gang-code indoctrination; it is far more deeply an indictment of the pervasive sham, fakery, and deviousness upon which the whole society is built. And the emptiness with which Bruno accepts his tribe's mass violation of the only person who has offered him warmth and trust is not evidence that his conscience is dead, nor is the cavalier swagger which he affects as he walks up and down the long line of rapists who are waiting like customers in the express lane at a supermarket. Indeed, at a moment when Sheeny Louie is more concerned about glass in the street than about the crime he is waiting to commit, Bruno's failure to accept the enormity of his betrayal is a common psychological defense. Algren's treatment here is very like Ernest Hemingway's practice of signalizing matters of consuming importance by saying as little as possible about them.

The quickening of the individual conscience as a result of acts performed under the destructive force of environment is characteristic of the guilt motif in Algren's novels. Were Bruno totally subservient to his environment, like his fellow Division-Streeters, he could feel no pangs. Emotionally an outsider, he is capable of harboring a burden typical of sophisticated societies — the sense of guilt. From the moment of his retreat from the dark hole under the sidewalk, he is "checking a rising dread by feigning a toughness to himself that he could not feel"; and, despite his capitulation to the gang law, he is emotionally scarred by Steffi's hard and cryptic challenge of "Next! Next!" that is uttered in a laugh that is like a sob. Bruno releases his unbearable tension by murdering the Greek line-crasher, whom he catches unfairly with arms entangled in coat sleeves; but later, in a daydream prizefight, he declines to take similar advantage of his opponent since "this Bicek wasn't one to take advantage of man, woman, or child."

Thereafter, Bruno, to the moment when he tries to redeem both himself and Steffi by an escape plan and a marriage proposal, is guilt-ridden. He assumes guilt for shooting an old man, not so much out of a semi-heroic adherence to the underworld fiat against "squealing" as from a secret yearning to be punished for "what he had made of Steffi R. He had snuck off with a bottle in his hand while the one human he loved had been turned into a loveless thing. And there was in his nature, so deep it had never before been sounded, the conviction that no punishment was too great for such a betrayal." Indeed, he wishes that he were actually guilty of the shooting in order to have a crime for which he could suffer compensatory punishment. But he knows, too, that there is no atonement for an act so unpardonable. In the moral murder represented by his betrayal of Steffi, "he had killed Steffi in his heart" just as surely as he alone had killed the Greek. Therefore, though no atonement is possible, he will suffer punishment for both crimes.

In *Never Come Morning*, Algren for the first time crystallizes the relationship between love and death which, with some variation, lies at the center of all his novels. Only hinted at in *Somebody in Boots*, when Cass McKay thoughtlessly but prophetically charges his sister to become a prostitute, the relationship becomes full-blown thereafter. George Bluestone has rightly noticed that "in Algren's central vision, self-destruction becomes operative only after the destruction of some loved object. The moment a central character becomes responsible for such ruin, he is irrevocably doomed. That 'irrational, destructive force' then, is the impulse to destroy love which is tantamount to death."[11]

VI   *Style and Symbols*

Algren's peculiar strength as a Naturalistic novelist, however, resides in the method by which he presents and develops his basic themes. Rejecting the "drab, coal-smoky style"[12] of the Emile Zola tradition, Algren treats his material with Whitmanesque self-identification, compassion, and poetic vision. Symbolism and figurative language lend his prose a poetic mood and a suggestive power sufficiently pervasive to make his novels much more than "little encyclopedias of off-beat information, unprinted articles from a scandalous *National Geographic*."[13] The minuteness and accuracy of Algren's observations provide an unquestionable sense of authority, but he avoids "the tedium of the naturalistic stereotype, of the literal copying of surfaces. He knows how to select, how to employ factual details without letting himself be swamped by them."[14] In *Never Come Morning*, the basic ingredients of Algren's technique coalesce to produce a novel in which, as one critic could say, "the poetry and feeling . . . [make] this story, even though the tale is of low louts without decency."[15]

Never Come Morning, then, is the first major work in which "Algren's characteristic symbolism and indirection endow the action with pity and concealed prophecy."[16] With its single setting and homogeneous cast of characters, the imagery and symbolism are more closely integrated with mood and theme than in *Somebody in Boots*. Rain is a recurrent mood-setter, as in the earlier novel; but, instead of reflecting the protagonist's sense of imminent death, it evokes an all-encompassing air of futility and hopelessness that begins with Mama Bicek's extra-sensory perception of doom in the commencement of an all-night rain at the moment her son begins his career as a hoodlum.

The by now familiar images of mutilation appear in the picture of "a bleeding heart in an oval frame" and in the futile scrambling of a wingless fly during the first act of ritualistic love-making which officially inaugurates the love affair between Bruno and Steffi. Bruno's beheading of Steffi's Charlie McCarthy doll is reminiscent of Bryan's vicious decapitation of the housecat in *Somebody in Boots*. Just as Dove Linkhorn of *A Walk on the Wild Side* regards the fairy-tale tin soldier as his counterpart, Bruno recognizes the grinning doll as a taunting symbol of all the stuffed things which will be his only rewards in the boxing ring and on the baseball diamond of his life.

VII   *Theme and Structure*

Imagery, symbolism, and general tone combine to support the titular theme. Algren remembers that *Never Come Morning* was not his original title but the suggestion of an editor. Lawrence Lipton says, "Algren's title was originally the working title of my own book and I relinquished it to him at the suggestion of our mutual editor at Harper."[17] The words that make up the title do appear, however, in a climactic scene when Bruno tries but fails to speak his remorse to Steffi. He leaves her, saying, "I don't trust nobody. Not even myself no more. I don't trust nothin'." Afterward, as Steffi lies beside the barber, she dreams that she is the victim of an all-night search during which she has "to hide, and forever in some degrading posture: on all fours in the alley behind the poolroom, between the telephone poles and an open refuse can." Though the hunter knows her hiding place, he prolongs the search, knowing, perhaps, as Steffi does, "that the night would be forever, the lamps would never fade, the taverns never close, morning would never come again." A significant variation of the phrase appears when Bruno himself regains consciousness in One-Eye Tenczara's query room: "someone had pulled the window shade, shutting the morning out forever; as though, in this room, no morning was ever wanted."

Supporting the central theme is Algren's structural device which Chester Eisinger has called "the tactic of the false dawn"[18] — a technique of leading trapped characters through their seemingly eternal night to the glimmering of a bright dawn, only to have the saving light turn suddenly to the death-darkness for which their lives have been programmed from the beginning. In *Never Come Morning*, the marriage compact between Bruno and Steffi, made in defiance of the barber's blackmail, provides a vision of release into the promise of true dawn. But the single sunlit moment of Steffi's life, when she feels for the first time that "everything was going to be all right after all," is the moment which insures that she will spend the rest of her life in the dark night of the soul.

Critics have disagreed about the structure of *Never Come Morning*. To Eisinger, for instance, the tale is "only fitfully plotted" and contains "only enough narrative material for a short story."[19] The brothel and police line-up scenes appear tangential to Eisinger. George Bluestone, however, says that, following the rape of Steffi, Algren proves "a master of digression" in creating "three broad sequences: Bruno's apprehension and imprisonment; Steffi's life as a prostitute; Bruno's ring battle with Honeyboy Tucker. The first is essentially comic, the second poignantly subjective, the third graphically descriptive."[20] Whatever the nature of these sequences, they cannot be divorced from the main theme and purpose of the story. Each develops some aspect of the intertwined lives of Bruno and Steffi; each amplifies the condition of their lives at that point in the narrative; and, above all, each heightens the prevailing mood and increases the significance of the basic theme. In these important respects, the sequences are not tangential or separate entities; they are essential components of the narrative.

All three sequences are presented with authority and vitality — and often with subtlety and poignancy. In *Never Come Morning*, Algren elevates the early deposition technique of "So Help Me" to the drama of the interrogation and line-up scenes. Bruno becomes part of the ceaseless procession of underworld figures who are under the jurisdiction of Captain One-Eye Tenczara, the immediate literary progenitor of the haunted Record-Head Bednar of *The Man with the Golden Arm*. Though the interrogations of Bruno are in the framework of the popular detective-novel "third degree," they transcend the worn stereotype through their deeper social significance and through complex shifts of tone and pacing from pointed irrelevancies to exchanges of grim quip until both Bruno and Tenczara appear to be "caught in a game which neither understands and yet which each must play."[21] In the long scene interpolated between interrogations, Bruno takes his place among the netherworld parasites whose unction or incorrigibility have made Tenczara the ultimate sceptic.

Algren's years of devoted attendance upon the actual line-ups must have supplied the following spectrum of the lower depths for this novel: the veteran who prowls the streets with artillery concealed under his clothes; "Ready-Money," the young Negro car-prowler who is already under parole; the eighteen-year-old, red-haired Dane who leaves a jimmy in a gas-station door without criminal intent; Murray Taub, who has "beat society out of four hundred years" in penal institutions; the blond boy in his early twenties, for whom "any Tuesday afternoon in cloudland was once upon a time"; the forty-year-old dwarf who taps gas mains and gets boosted through transoms; and many more who supply outlandish, transparent, half-hearted alibis. Among them, Hardrocks O'Connor, the hardest of them all, with ten solid pages of crime to show for his life, weeps openly, sobbing to unseen faces, "I can't make it no more." In graduating from vandalism to hoodlumhood, Bruno has become one of these. This appearance in the line-up is his commencement ceremony.

The brothel scenes of Steffi's captivity at Mama Tomek's are Algren's first venture into the chintz-and-brocade parlors for which, later, in *A Walk on the Wild Side*, he was to become known as America's foremost literary spokesman. In these curtained rooms where morning never comes, where each girl has been with a hundred men in a hundred corners, where Coca Cola is both a beverage and standard professional equipment, and where both minutes and towels are counted to the jingle of the slot machine and the jangle of the jukebox, the life of the housegirl unrolls with a verisimilitude and understanding seldom achieved in fiction. Only William Faulkner, among twentieth-century writers, has caught a similar blend of the comic, the grotesque, and the faintly sinister in his scenes at the house of Miss Reba in *Sanctuary*, *The Mansion*, and *The Reivers*; but even he has not captured the poignancy of Algren's vignettes.

In the relentless war with police, Mama Tomek's girls have only two fears: "the Heat" and disease. In a succession of penetrating character sketches, each girl reveals her pathetic dreams and aspirations, her special talents and failings, and her peculiar fetishes and borderline insanities. Over this temple of alternate boredom and frenzy, of blended hilarity and despair, presides the imperturbable Mama Tomek, who periodically sniffs through a nostril-straw her cones of narcotic powder and who hypnotically recites her life story to the half-witted houseboy, Snipes, who hears it afresh each time, as if it is a bedtime story. Yet, in her narcotic haze, Mama Tomek justifies all city wilderness survival tactics: "It's just like you try to walk straight down a crooked alley — you'll bump your puss on a barn or fall over somethin' for sure. That's how ever'thin' is, Snipey — ever'thin's crooked so you got to walk crooked." Her contention that morals are only "a act dames got to have to defend theirselves with" is warrant for Chicadee's defense of whoredom which later becomes a rationale of *A Walk on the Wild Side:* prostitution makes better sense than scrubbing floors or slicing bacon because "the lower the wage the greater the morality demanded of you off the job."

The concluding boxing bout sequence between Bruno and Honeyboy Tucker is climactic and crucial. Upon the outcome of this contest hangs everything of importance in the story, not only the future of the two main characters but also the affirmation or negation of the theme of ethnic and environmental entrapment. The simultaneous victory and defeat of Bruno is a clear and forceful answer: a demonstration that the potential to climb above the jungle is ultimately not enough to disentangle the web of circumstance which is even stronger than championship form.

The prizefight sequences, moreover, are the device by which Algren creates the first structural circular treatment in his novels, a form which has been discussed as characteristic of the later novel, *A Walk on the Wild Side*. The story is framed between the opening prizefight in which Casey Benkowski dutifully follows the barber's orders by "taking a dive" and the concluding sequence in which Bruno's almost superhuman stamina in the prize-ring is a direct revolt against all the "crooked business" reflected in Casey's doglike devotion to underworld edict. Algren's narrative talents are more than equal to the sheer narrative power demanded by the crucial fight scene. In fact, the spare, tight rendering of every feint, every bob and weave, every legitimate and illegitimate tactic, and every thought and sensation during more than eight rounds of action reveals a narrative sense which could have made Algren a superlative writer of sports fiction.[22]

Despite the superficially episodic appearance of these sequences, they are not detached from the main narrative stream. On the contrary, *Never Come Morning* has a special importance in Algren's development because it demonstrates his capacity to go beyond the "road story" in order to weave a tale with "a remarkably integrated approach to his theme."[23]

VIII *Critical Reception: Furor at Home; Understanding Abroad*

When the story of Lefty Bicek appeared, it spawned a literary whirlwind. Richard Wright's introduction, which highlighted the sociological implications and the effectiveness of Algren's talent for blending poetry with realism, led critics and reviewers to notice the similarities between *Never Come Morning* and *Native Son* and to say, among other things, that Bruno appeared to be "a sort of Polish-American Bigger Thomas."[24] Poles in Chicago regarded the tale of Bruno Bicek as a perverse and intolerable slur upon all Polish-Americans. In later editions of *Never Come Morning*, Algren provides a preface which reviews this onslaught that began with the unsuccessful request from the Polish Roman Catholic Union that the publishers remove the novel from circulation because it "fosters national disunity" during a time of war. He quotes extensively from attacks in the Polish daily paper *Zgoda* which opened a second front against the book and its author by proclaiming Algren to be "a product of distorted mentality" who could not "possibly be without malice in his heart against the Poles."

Though the furor was strong enough to keep the novel off the shelves of the Chicago Public Library for several years, it is there now; and Algren finds satisfaction in the high regard which the story enjoys outside Chicago, especially abroad. In one of the bizarre literary accidents which have characterized Algren's career, a French journalist who knew "some schoolroom English" translated *Never Come Morning* into what emerged as almost unreadable kindergarten prose; but Jean-Paul Sartre's good French translation later prompted other translations in many languages and made this Chicago "neighborhood novel" more widely read in Europe than in America. So, observes Algren in his later preface, "The novel that the rear-echelon patriots and Sunday-morning Forgive-Me-Lords failed to understand strangely has found understanding on the bookshelves of Europe. *Le matin se fait attendre*, Jean-Paul Sartre's translation, was the first of a dozen translations. It is now available in every large city from London to Tokyo, Rio to Zagreb."

CHAPTER 5

The Dead End Of Lost Chance:
The Man With The Golden Arm

S EVEN years after the publication of *Never Come Morning*, the more sensational and more widely acclaimed novel, *The Man with the Golden Arm* (1949), appeared. Returning from the war to the Division-Street neighborhood, Algren had subjected himself to the rigors of creating a "significant" American novel:

The way I wrote *The Man with the Golden Arm* was to live very austerely, because in order to finish a book you have to have the energy — not only the energy of a cat, but you have to go every day and you can't do it over weekends. As soon as you lose a day, you lose. There's no such thing as standing still. You've got to push — keep pushing — a book, and you can't do anything else. I can't. It means giving up a lot of things. It means you've got to believe in writing strongly enough, you know, to say, "Now, don't bother me. I'm not going to the track. I'm not going to gamble. I'm going to bed at nine o'clock, get up at five and work'til eight, then go to the YMCA, or something, and work out, then get back and work in the afternoon. And that's it."[1]

And that was "it" for the better part of two years, during which time he received two grants — the Newberry Library Award of $2000 (1947) and a stipend of $1000 from the American Academy of Arts and Letters (1947). Moreover, he was working under a publisher's agreement which provided sixty dollars a week for two years. With this financial help, he was able to complete the manuscript in time to spend the summer of 1949 in Europe before the book appeared that fall.

I   *Thematic Evolution: From War to Narcotics*

The story was not originally conceived as a tale about drug addiction nor even as a "Chicago novel." In fact, it underwent a three-phase evolution before it emerged in the fall of 1949 to become eventually the first winner (1950) of the National Book Award as well as the basis for a motion picture (1956) which crashed the long-standing taboo against narcotics as a subject for popular films. Algren's original arrangement with his publishers called for a war novel, but he soon discovered that "if you don't do a thing while you're there — at least the way I operate — you can't do it. It slips away. Two months after the war it was gone; . . . and this thing just got more real; I mean the neighborhood I was living in, and these people, were a lot more real than the army was."[2]

As a result, Algren turned again to the Division-Street neighborhood people — many the same ones he had known while writing *Never Come Morning* — and to a novel built around the life of a neighborhood card dealer. He worked on this story for nearly two years before he met a drug addict; and not realizing, at first, that the addict and his other new friends were heavily "on the needle," he found himself accepted as a gratuitous, non-participating member of the drug scene. When he submitted his manuscript about the card dealer to his agent, she suggested that the story "needed a peg; it didn't seem to be hung on anything."[3] Not until then did it occur to Algren that the "peg" might come from what he had learned about the circle of friends with whom he spent evenings listening to jazz music. This afterthought became the most dramatic, in some ways the most significant, and the most sensational aspect of the new novel.

Though *The Man with the Golden Arm* retains the general locale and the social levels of *Never Come Morning*, there are significant differences between the two books. The world of *Never Come Morning* is a young people's world, and the story revolves around the internal quests and external conflicts of a seventeen-year-old Polish couple. In *The Man With the Golden Arm*, Frankie Machine and Sophie, nearly thirty years old, have survived the baptismal years of their society and are long beyond the first golden flush of the success-vision. Their prime enemy now is the deadly boredom of the running-in-one-place life and the inexorable fading of the Dream. Their suffering already has a history that is a slow and tortuous prelude to their inevitable demise.

Francis Majcinek, known along West Division Street as Frankie Machine in recognition of the mechanical efficiency with which he deals the nightly card game at Zero Schwiefka's, is a twenty-nine-year-old army veteran who has been in an evacuation hospital with a shard of shrapnel in his liver. Before the war, he had already made his name as the most reliable dealer on the street and had formed a curiously close friendship with "the punk," Sparrow "Solly" Saltskin, who describes himself as "half Hebe 'n half crazy." As "steerer" at the door of Schwiefka's gambling room, Sparrow had remembered Frankie and had yearned for his homecoming while others had forgotten him. Now, together again, "the tranquil, square-faced, shagheaded little buffalo-eyed blond called Frankie Machine and the ruffled, jittery punk called Sparrow felt they were about as sharp as the next pair of hustlers." While Sparrow goggles at Frankie's dexterity with corny parlor-game card tricks and numbers gags, Frankie is secretly flattered by the punk's admiration and devotion.

But, though beyond Sparrow's comprehension, things are not the same as they were before. How can Sparrow know that, beside shrapnel in the liver, Frankie has also come home with a "monkey on his back," one grown there by the morphine which deadens the pain of his wound? Frankie's is only a small monkey, but the neighborhood "fixer," Nifty Louie Fomorowsky, knows that Frankie, like all the rest, will soon graduate from "student" to "junkie" with a thirty-five-pound monkey, and that he will consume a quarter-grain of morphine a day and gain weight. Helping the monkey's growth, too, is Frankie's other burden: Sophie, his wife of ten years, who had married him by means of a false pregnancy and who has since been crippled in an auto accident that occurred when Frankie drank while driving. Though doctors find nothing physically wrong with Sophie, she now waits for Frankie at home; she is wheelchair-bound with a deep psychosomatic illness. Because of Frankie's sense of guilt, which she fervently nourishes and perpetuates, she keeps him always morally and spiritually in her debt.

The world of Frankie, Sophie, and Sparrow the punk is largely that of the neighborhood which revolves about the Division Arms Hotel, the Tug & Maul Bar, the Club Safari, and Zero Schwiefka's gambling room. In the Division Arms Hotel, upstairs above the rooms occupied by Frankie and Sophie, live "old husband" Stash Koskoska and his sensuous young wife, Vi. While the slow-witted old man works doggedly at the icehouse all day and lives only to bring home to Vi some cut-rate bargain in bread or Polish sausage, Vi lets Sparrow the punk eat the sausages and "make hurried love to her" in the apartment. When she is not entertaining the punk, Vi is attentive to the crippled Sophie; she cleans her apartment, wheels her about, and often takes her to double-feature movies. The landlord himself prowls the stairs, demands that all doors (except Vi's) be kept closed, incessantly hammers a loose stair which is never fixed, and pampers a half-witted son who plants paper daisies in the cracks of the staircase.

At the Tug & Maul, the hub of the multifarious activities of the neighborhood, all the well-known characters of this section of Division Street gather; and the "Owner" is a central clearinghouse for neighborhood news. A strange sort of zoo, the denizens of the Tug & Maul are Nifty Louie Fomorowsky, the local dope-pusher, the "Fixer," with his two-tone shoes; Drunkie John, "a mouth at the end of a whisky glass," a man permanently drunk who has never discovered who he is and has "tried nothing but whisky. A process which left him feeling like somebody new every day"; Molly Novotny, a pretty girl "scarcely out of her teens," who hustles drinks at the Safari to support Drunkie John; Meter Reader, baseball coach for the Endless Belt and Leather Invincibles; Zygmunt the Prospector, a disbarred lawyer, now calling himself a "claim adjuster"; Umbrella Man, who walks the streets tinkling a bell and wearing an umbrella strapped to his back; and that most abysmally offensive creature in Algren's fiction, Blind Pig (called Piggy-O), a refuse-heap specimen to whom "light and cleanliness were inseparable: if he could not have the one he would do without the other."

For the "reliable barflies" at the Tug & Maul, who are proud of their tavern's honest and unaffected atmosphere, the Club Safari across the street is an establishment almost beneath contempt. The Safari calls itself a "club" and serves mixed drinks "wit' leaves on top," which themselves bespeak the effete character of the place. Above the Club Safari is Louie's room to which the thirty-five-pound monkeys regularly drive all the neighborhood junkies. On certain afternoons before card games begin at Schwiefka's, the Dealer Frankie Machine slips secretly into this room for the "fix" which will insure "the steady hand and steady eye" of the expert card dealer. Unless he feels the *whan* of the shot, he becomes so ill that "nobody can stand gettin' that sick 'n live." To escape the oppression of his whimpering, nagging, half-demented wife, he has turned to the compulsive affection of Molly Novotny, whom Drunkie John has abandoned. With Molly Frankie finds a partial substitute for morphine: "It would be Molly-O or a quarter-grain fix, he'd never make it alone."

While Sophie sits in her wheelchair and broods over her *Scrap-*

book of Fatal Accidence, Frankie finds solace in the arms of Molly downstairs; and the bizarre "internal triangle" of Sparrow, Vi, and old Stash becomes more and more complicated upstairs. As Sparrow the punk shuttles into and out of jail for a variety of petty crimes, Frankie's habit grows, despite the ministrations of Molly-O: " 'Frankie's in the switches,' the punk brooded, 'it's like he wants to run somewheres 'n can't make up his mind which way to head.' "

But events at Schwiefka's bring Frankie's "switches" to a climax. Continuing to deal the fast, clean game upon which his reputation is founded, and trusting "no man on the other side of the slot," Frankie catches Louie the Fixer cheating the Umbrella Man and exposes the hand which Louie has called falsely. The Fixer's subsequent grudge against the Dealer brings tension to the poker games and raises the price of Frankie's weekly fix. Later, an altercation over Louie's lucky Silver Dollar, which Frankie refuses to exchange after the Fixer loses it gambling, leads to a confrontation in the alley. Sparrow, who is keeping the lucky piece for Frankie, drops it deliberately, and Louie bends to retrieve it. Frankie, in need of a fix, locks his fingers to control their sudden shaking and brings them down upon Louie with all his weight behind his coupled fists; and the Fixer's neck "flopped forward like a hen's with the ax half through it."

From that moment until Frankie regains awareness in a bowling alley — when Sparrow tells him that the Fixer's body is hidden in Schwiefka's alley woodshed — his mind has been so blank that he marvels, "I didn't even hear him fall." As they return to the card game, Sparrow whispers their alibi: "I'm glad that we were havin' coffee when that guy Fomorowsky Whatever His Name Is got slugged next door." Back at the card table, Frankie notices that Blind Pig, who was present during the initial quarrel, is no longer in the room.

Hereafter, Frankie Machine is the victim of a double chase; he is hounded by the police Captain Record-Head Bednar and pursued by the starving monkey on his back. At a New Year's party, Cousin Kvorka pointedly tells Frankie that a coroner's inquest will prove that The Fixer died of a broken neck. Though Frankie feigns innocence, he goes directly to Molly — the girl he "comes to when he's scared" — and confesses his guilt to her. She offers to run away with him when the time comes; but, when she warns him that Sparrow the punk has been seen spending large amounts of money at the Safari, Frankie suspects that Sparrow had taken Louie's large

bankroll while hiding the body and that his lavish spending will give
Bednar the evidence he needs. Sparrow's insistence that the money
is old Stash's Christmas bonus seems too convenient to be convincing. There is, however, another possibility: Blind Pig has appeared
in a new suit and is sitting in the Safari buying drinks "like he owns
the joint." Could Piggy-O be the culprit instead of the punk? Uncertain, Frankie suspects both, while he is fighting off the monkey with
Molly and whisky.

In the boredom of helpless waiting, Frankie and the punk steal
electric irons from Nieboldt's. The punk disappears in the crowds,
but Frankie is caught and convicted. The eight months in jail prove
for Frankie to be an "iron sanctuary" where "for a while, at least, all
things would be solved for him." There, with the help of the testy
prison doctor, he makes the long trip "from monkey to zero." The
only news from outside comes from Molly's single visit when he
learns that she has left the Safari and the apartment and that old
Stash has died in a fall from an open window.

Back on the street, free of guilt and rid of the habit, Frankie finds
that Molly has "drifted into the vast web of backstreet and
alleyway." Otherwise, "all things remained the same; yet all things
had changed." Hurt by the punk's leaving him to serve the jail
sentence alone, Frankie rejects Sparrow. He finds that his "touch"
with cards is gone and leaves the table in frustration, insults his old
friend Antek, begins to rely heavily on the needle, and at last settles
for Sparrow's old job as steerer for another dealer at Schwiefka's.

Circumstances close rapidly upon Frankie and the punk.
Unknown to Sparrow, Record-Head Bednar has guessed a way to
solve the murder of Louie, which has become a crucial political
issue. Putting Blind Pig on the payroll in order to get the punk, Bednar arranges for Pig to hire the destitute Sparrow to make a delivery
of junk. Sparrow does not know until the door opens that Frankie is
the buyer; and, according to Bednar's plan, the planted officers
catch both Frankie and Sparrow with the goods. As a user, Frankie is
released; but, as a pusher, the punk is retained on high bond.

Frankie desperately searches for Molly, who hides him for three
weeks in her apartment and supports his habit on love and codeine
until Drunkie John finds them. Angered by Drunkie's brutal
blackmailing of Molly, Frankie orders him away. Before Frankie and
Molly can get out of the apartment, John has sent the police; and
Frankie attempts to escape with a bullet in his heel, but is cornered
in a cheap flophouse where he hangs himself from the wire mesh

ceiling of his partitioned cubicle. The final report upon the life and death of Frankie Machine is given jointly by Antek Witwicki, Molly Novotny, and investigating officer Fallon at the coroner's inquest. "The case is closed."

II *Frankie Machine: His Arm Was Gold*

Algren found the title of the book and a key to the character of Frankie Machine in the war experiences which were to have been background material for the novel he had originally intended to write. Among his buddies during his army years had been a little Italian Blue Island bookie:

> He would yell, suddenly, "Fade me" and then he'd roll the dice — anywhere, even on the taut blanket of an army cot! Real quick. For a while he was lucky, but his luck reversed soon and he couldn't make a single point.
> He was always looking for a backer. "The arm's gold," he'd say, "Can't miss because it's gold." Then when he'd lose he'd cuss like hell.[4]

The golden-armed dice player became the card dealer with un-shakable faith in his arm and the dexterity and gaming sense to sub-stantiate that faith. The artistic transposition of dice player to card dealer was an obvious one; Algren, who has been an inveterate card player, had already proved himself competent as both amateur and professional dealer by the time he was writing this book. During his early years as an author, he ran a Saturday night poker game in his flat; and, when in the army, he "ran an acey-deucey game on a blanket all the way across France." But the idea for creating "the Dealer" as his hero came to him while he was dealing at the Lucky Star tavern across from his apartment on Wabansia Avenue in Chicago and was thinking about writing his new book.[5]

Frankie had first appeared in print, however, in a poem, an epitaph published in *Poetry: A Magazine of Verse* in September, 1947. According to Algren, the poem preceded the book in conception as well as in publication.

Epitaph: The Man with the Golden Arm

It's all in the wrist, with a deck or a cue,
And Frankie Machine had the touch
He had the touch, and a golden arm —
"Hold up, Arm," he would plead,
kissing his rosary once for help

with the faders sweating it out and
Zing! — there it was — Little Joe or Eighter from Decatur
Double-trey the hard way, dice be nice,
When you get a hunch bet a bunch
It don't mean a thing if it don't cross that string
Tell 'em where you got it 'n how easy it was —
We remember Frankie Machine
And the arm that always held up.

We remember in the morning light
When the cards are boxed and the long cues racked
Straight up and down like the all-night hours
With the hot rush-hour past.

For it's all in the wrist with a deck or a cue
And if he crapped out when we thought he was due
it must have been that the dice were rolled
for he had the touch, and his arm was gold:
Rack up his cue, give the steerer his hat,

The arm that held up has failed at last.
Yet why does the light down the dealer's slot
Sift soft as light in a troubled dream?
(A dream, they say, of a golden arm
that belonged to the dealer we called Machine.)

Like most of Algren's heroes, Frankie, as developed in the novel, is not so much flawed in the classic sense as deprived in the modern. Like Bruno Bicek, he inhabits a jungle where toughness is necessary for survival; yet Sparrow the punk is "the only hustler on Division Street who still believed there was anything tough about Frankie Machine. The times he had seen Frankie back down just didn't count for Sparrow." But the time comes when Frankie backs down even to the punk. Further, Frankie, from his youth, has lacked discrimination in his judgment of people: "It hadn't seemed to make any difference to him whether he dated a schoolgirl, a nurse, a dimwit, a shimmy dancer, a hill-billy, an aging whore, a divorcee or just some poor tired tramp." Therefore Sophie's query is pertinent: "How could anyone make a fellow like that ashamed of himself?" Even when Frankie sees himself clearly for what he is, his perception has no shame, only a form of mild regret: "Ain't nobody scared of me my whole life." He places too little value on himself to be capable of shame, which is not to say that he is incapable of guilt and regret.

III   *Guilt: Universal and Personal*

Frankie's sense of guilt is the hub of the most intricate pattern of guilt motifs in all of Algren's fiction: his is individual and personalized guilt enclosed by generalized and impersonal guilt. A common guilt of all dispossessed and disinherited in American society at large is the guilt of non-ownership: "the great, secret, and special American guilt of owning nothing, nothing at all, in the one land where ownership and virtue are one." This guilt is the burden of all those from any quarter who end on the Great American Skid Row where "even the native-born no longer felt they had been born in America. They felt they had merely emerged from the wrong side of its billboards."

In *The Man with the Golden Arm,* however, the common guilt of the accused doubles back upon the accuser. To Police Captain Record-Head Bednar, whose life has been an endless cataloging of the guilty, his mission of capture and condemnation has become a special form of guilt. The pervasiveness of guilt is established early in the first few paragraphs when Bednar cannot sleep because he is conscious of guilt as the Heritage of Man, almost an adjunct of Original Sin: "The city had filled him with the guilt of others; he was numbed by his charge sheet's accusations." Thus, as a kind of receiving center, Bednar becomes the interpreter of all men's guilt. Stabbed by his recognition of the universal truth in the concept that "everybody's a habitual in his heart," Bednar is driven to the larger premise that "those whom he had denied, those beyond the wall, had all along been members of himself." If so, each man's guilt is the guilt of all men. None can escape. Therefore Bednar, as the Recording Angel of all men, scrawls across the record-sheet of mankind that most terrifying ultimate judgment found on this side of St. Peter's gate: *Guilty.*

In a real sense, *The Man with the Golden Arm* is the unmasking of one man's guilt and the tracing of the causes and consequences of that guilt. Just as each man must accept the burden of his own special guilt, Frankie Machine must bear what he has allotted to himself: the overbearing consciousness that through his negligence his wife has become a totally dependent cripple. The accident "had truly married them at last. For where her love and the Church's ritual had failed to bind, guilt had now drawn the irrevocable knot so fiercely that she felt he could never be free of her again." The yearning for punishment which is a concomitant of Frankie's guilt, even after his jail sentence has been a substitute purge and has therefore offered him another chance, is the prime source of his need for the oblivion of the "fix." To Molly, just before Frankie experiences the last chase into the last lonely corner of his life, he sums up the urgency of his guilt:

"The troubles started pilin' up on me the day I got back in that room with Zosh," he remembered. "I didn't know how to get out from under 'n the more they piled up the more it felt like it was all my fault, right from the beginning, when me 'n Zosh was little stubs together 'n I made her do the things she wouldn't of done with nobody else. Whatever happened to me, it seemed like, was just somethin' I had comin' for a long time, I don't know why. It's why I rolled up all the little troubles into one big trouble."

For Frankie Machine the "one big trouble" is the insatiable, morphine-fed monkey riding on his back all the way into the "dead end of lost chance."

But Frankie has had the chance to win as well as to lose. In a life dominated by games and numbers, the ironies of luck have been as felicitous as perverse. Though Frankie's first dependence upon narcotics may have come from circumstances he could not control, it is both ironic and apt that the jail term which temporarily delivers him from that dependence is legal retribution for one of the real crimes for which he feels no guilt. He has no remorse for either the theft of merchandise or the murder of Louie; but, like Bruno Bicek who seeks punishment because he has "murdered Steffi in his heart," Frankie feels that, somehow, his jail sentence for theft has helped rid him of guilt for murdering Sophie in his heart. His return to the oppressiveness of that guilt pierces him where he has no armor, and his return to morphine causes the loss of all his chances at once and forever.

For Frankie, there has been at least the shadow of redemption. He seeks and finds it ephemerally in the arms of Molly Novotny. He finds it temporarily through the scarification of the soul represented by time in jail. But, ironically, the only effective self-punishment is also his destroyer; and the man he murders, the Fixer himself, tries to tell him so while Frankie is yet a "student": "When I hear a junkie tell me he wants to kick the habit but he just can't I know he lies even if *he* don't know he does. He *wants* to carry the monkey, he's punishin' hisself for somethin' 'n don't even know it."

For Frankie Machine, even these are avenues of self-castigation and of possible redemption; but for the haunted Captain Bednar, no redemption exists anywhere. Like Frankie, he has come to know that "All debts had to be paid. Yet for his own there was no currency."

With all men's guilt heaped upon his head, Bednar can find no release: "thieves, embezzlers and coneroos, all might redeem themselves in time. But for himself, who had played the spiritual con game, there was no such redemption." For Record-Head Bednar has denied himself in denying the convict and the prostitute; and, in rejecting them, the Captain has cut himself off from communion with humanity. He no longer has a place among men, for he is guilty of much the same Unforgiveable Sin which Nathaniel Hawthorne's Ethan Brand found in his own heart.

Algren's use of the guilt motif, which achieves its fullest and most complex exploration in *The Man with the Golden Arm*, also becomes most intimately involved with the "advancement of the love-death theme"[6] which had appeared in two previous novels but which becomes Algren's main concern here. The significant advance in the relationship between guilt and the love-death theme lies largely in the heightened subtlety and complexity of Algren's depiction of women.

IV   *Complex, Credible Women*

In no previous story had Algren created women characters with such intensity or psychological insight. Molly Novotny is the least complex. Though not a professional prostitute, this small dark-haired girl "scarcely out of her teens," with a heart-shaped face and "eyes dark with exhaustion," has all the strangely tender passivity, the innate generosity, and the capacity for indiscriminate affection which has been typical of the literary version of the Whore with a Heart of Gold. During her initial scene, when Drunkie John abuses her and degrades her far beyond ordinary human endurance, Antek the Owner says of her, "She got too big a heart, that girl. A guy can walk into her heart with army boots on."

Molly "had never understood why she had lived with a man like Drunkie John, for whom she cared nothing at all, and found the answer now: when a woman feels useless, she doesn't think anything of throwing herself away. One way of doing it, with one man or another, was as good a way as any other then." In a recent letter, Algren wrote "Molly's hangups are those, no more and no less, of any woman anyone might meet, in any bar, anywhere: she doesn't have a craft, she's lonely, she wants to survive." She is, however, in most respects the antithesis of Sophie. Consequently, to a man like Frankie, who is decimated by Sophie's relentless psychological bullying, Molly poses absolutely no threat; she offers instead acceptance, understanding, and comfort. Frankie's gravitation toward Molly is inevitable, as Sophie knows in her desperation; but she can only vent her spleen in her constant reference to Molly as "that piece of trade downstairs."

Sophie, the most subtle study of woman in Algren's fiction, is the richest product of his conviction that women are more interesting than men and offer more to the novelist: "The only men interesting to write about are, say, fighters — or jockeys. The average middle-class American man isn't interesting. The women are. Women always have something more going. . . . They're more dramatic." Algren considers Sophie his most memorable woman character. "I don't particularly like her," he says, "but she comes to life."

Her credibility results, largely, from her destructive compulsions. It is too easy and too simple merely to tag her, as many have done, as a selfish and vindictive woman. She is, rather, a monstrous but pathetic psychological cripple; and she is driven to perpetual hypochondriac hysteria by her possessive dependence upon a man inferior by class and education but superior in his self-confidence and sheer indifference. His indifference becomes a challenge to her pride, which, in turn, makes holy wedlock an unholy war of possession — a war which she is destined to lose since Frankie has never really cared for her.

When as teenagers Frankie had casually cast Sophie loose in order to be free to "play the field," she had launched a lifetime crusade to regain her lost pride through the only weapon at her command: a total psychological domination over him through his sense of guilt. "For that had been the endless pity of it: she had loved the clown. She had loved him in that curtained corner of her mind where, unknown to herself, she had planned an ultimate reckoning." The accident, which provided the cause for her psychosomatic paralysis, proved to be the solution to the single obsessive drive of her existence. It served the same purpose as the false pregnancy which had forced their wedlock; she had "gotten underneath his indifference. The hook was in." Her manic drive for possession and her psychological dominance are nothing so simple as mere vindictiveness, however. Her drive to dominate is fully as essential to her survival as Frankie's need to escape that domination is to him. And, when Frankie is lost at last, both to himself and to her, she disintegrates into a bundle of childish fantasies and is sent to a padded cell.

Besides Molly and Sophie, there is also Vi Koskoska. Sensuous and self-sufficient, emancipated from the Old-World subservience to men or custom, Vi uses her men to suit her whim and advantage. Because her "old husband," Stash, is basically a comic figure, almost one from the tradition of cuckoldry in the old fabliaux, he appears to deserve what would otherwise seem unconscionably bad treatment from his nubile young wife. His stupidity and self-concern hardly merit even pathos. Therefore, Vi suffers little loss of sympathy in her brash and often drunken sexual antics with the punk; and she does, in fact, somehow rise above all her men. Having found the punk no longer useful after the death of old Stash — "How could a girl afford a toy that never brought in a dime?" — she rids herself of him, marries her landlord, reforms herself and the beer-sodden hound Rumdum, becomes respectable, and begins to do good work in the community.

V *The Comic Scenes: A Humor of Compassion*

Few Algren critics have noticed that the comic scenes in *The Man with the Golden Arm* are the zenith of Algren's steady development toward a unique melding of the comic and the Naturalistic. In *Never Come Morning*, the comedy is lively and fitting but sporadic, since the prevailing mood is still the foreboding of death-consciousness which had characterized *Somebody in Boots;* on the other hand, the prevailing tone of *A Walk on the Wild Side* is comic. But, in *The Man with the Golden Arm*, these two moods paradoxically co-exist and even reinforce each other in creating the richness and verisimilitude of "the texture of urban experience"[7] for which this novel is unique among its kind.

In *The Man with the Golden Arm*, the comic scenes do more than serve as relief or leavening for serious matter; they illustrate the author's perception that there is something innately bizarre in even the most bitter and futile aspects of life in urban neighborhoods. In *The Man with the Golden Arm*, scenes which might appear wildly outlandish in another context are necessary to achieve the authentic savor of this particular mode of life. For this reason, Algren's highly specialized form of comedy, effective as comedy itself, also serves to intensify the mood of horror and foreboding rather than to diminish it.

Rumdum, the beer-sotted, wind-breaking, square-snapping "Polish Airedale," provides, for instance, a good deal more than burlesque humor. He is an integral part of a twilight world where all forms of life are affected by alcohol and narcotics. And, because he is the bestial counterpart of Drunkie John, Blind Pig, and even Frankie

Machine himself, he serves as a foil. It is ironic that Frankie should bring Rumdum to Sophie instead of the "puppy-pup" for whose affection she yearns; and it is even more ironic that, while Sophie and Frankie disintegrate through Frankie's increasing addiction, Rumdum should be so reformed as to need and want only milk and dog biscuits.

Indeed, the animals in *The Man with the Golden Arm* comprise a back-alley bestiary in which the purr of a bar-owner's cat[8] marks a man's decline into alcoholism and in which a treacherous dog, who eats the punk's hamburger and then bites his hand, is a kind of moral counterpart of Sparrow's betrayal of Frankie. However bitterly comic, all such elements — the soothsaying bar-cat, the dog-stealing and "scraunching" routes, the beer-hound Rumdum who reforms, the faithless dog who bites instead of letting himself be stolen — reinforce the theme that, though the back alleys themselves never change, "no sort of living [is] left" in them.

The domestic comedy supplied by Vi, Stash, and the punk is a travesty of married love and a direct inversion of Sophie's psychotic possessiveness. Though this comedy is often the broadest kind of bedroom farce, it is still a meaningful counterpoint to the desperation which characterizes the marriage of Sophie and Frankie. Therefore, the humor in Vi's cavalier treatment of her own marriage intensifies the tragic portent in Sophie's doomed struggle to perpetuate a marriage by entrapment.

In this novel, more than in Algren's others, comedy adds a dimension to the Determinism which rules life in the urban jungle. The key to its mood and function lies in the prefatory quotation from Alexandre Kuprin: "All the horror is in just this — that there is no horror." The comedy, then, is part of the horror which arises from lack of horror in a world where "woman is the downfall of every man and man is the downfall of every woman," where new ways of doing "will get you in trouble the same as the old ways," and where "neither God, war, nor the ward super work any great change." Among people forgotten even by the hustlers' God who "marked Sparrow's occasional fall," the cry of the anonymous girl being jailed — "Ain't anybody on *my* side?" — rings down all the jailhouse corridors of life with the plaintive humor whose edge of horror lies in the rhetorically negative answer. To Algren, the horror and the humor are inseparable. In discussing Federico Fellini's movie *La Dolce Vita*, Algren called this concept of comedy "a humor of compassion."[9]

VI   *Ethics and Values*

The system of ethics and values indigenous to the hustlers' society is specially adapted to justifying their way of life, and the basic tenet of this system is best phrased in Louie Fomorowsky's contention: "anything that pays ain't nothin' to be ashamed of." His practical viewpoint finds variants in Sparrow's belief that the hustler and the businessman are the same and in the ironic shift from Vi's rationalization that Sparrow's lies "are a poor man's pennies" to her rejection of him in favor of "landlord's nickels." For hustlers like Sparrow and Frankie, however, disaster lies in the hustlers' philosophy that even trouble is better than monotony.

When trouble breaks the monotony, the only salvation lies in the interdependence of people, all of whom, as Sophie perceives, have been "twisted about a bit, whether they sat in a wheelchair or not" — all the nameless people who "were bound . . . to the streets as the streets seemed bound to the night and the night to the nameless day." In time of trouble, one must trust those to whom one is bound, as Molly reminds Frankie when she says, "The way it is with you 'n me, when it ain't straight no more it's over." Yet trust to the hustler is no simple matter: trust demands a reciprocity of which the hustler himself may be incapable. Like Bruno Bicek, Frankie is robbed of faith in trust since he must pose the question "How could he expect anyone to trust him who could not trust himself?" Molly's penetration of Frankie's distrust is a major breakthrough and a harbinger of the "false dawn" upon which Frankie and Molly subsist until the end. Though Frankie had never trusted Sparrow or Sophie, he found in Molly the true reciprocity which could evoke his own; "for how does any man keep straight with himself if he has no one with whom to be straight?"

VII   *Images and Symbols: Crutches and Crosses*

In *The Man with the Golden Arm*, these motifs and values are dramatized through interrelated images and symbols, some adapted from previous stories but most devised for this novel alone. The image of boots from Algren's first novel reappears in the description of Molly as a girl whose heart "you can walk in 'n out of with boots on." This symbol of authority becomes the symbol of Frankie's prerogative to trample Molly's heart with "army brogans on his feet." The titular image from *Never Come Morning* is also adapted to describe the desperation with which card players unite "in unspoken conspiracy to stave off morning forever" because each player knows "that his life was reshuffled here with every hand."

Other symbols, which occur for the first time in this novel, represent motifs which Algren has used many times before. One is the cracked crutch which appears in Antek's bar just before the automobile accident and which inexplicably appears again in the closet of Sophie's hospital room shortly afterward. As a symbol of the crippling which evokes Frankie's guilt, the cracked crutch gains ironic force because Sophie, with no broken bones or other perceptible injury, becomes a psychosomatic cripple anyway. Another effective symbol, so recurrent as to be almost a motif, is the torn sleeve of Frankie's combat jacket. The sleeve is torn and frayed at moments when Frankie himself is torn; it is mended by some appropriate person or agency when Frankie is mended; and in death, the sleeve, like Frankie himself, is torn never to be mended again. Officer Fallon describes Frankie's death posture at the inquest: "He must have hit the bedpost with his forehead when the wire gave, it was bruised there where he hit it and tore the sleeve of his jacket." Perhaps the most effective single example of these symbols is that of the hunter and the hunted which is represented by the ceiling-high mural at Antek's of a hawk descending upon a duck. Frankie, of course, cannot avoid identifying himself with "the duck on the wall overhead."

The most successful imagery in this book, however, is the sustained symbolic presentation of various aspects of the guilt motif. George Bluestone has commented upon Algren's "inverted use of the Christian myth to comment ironically on the action" through the recurrent figure of the Cross, a figure which is ironic because "in Algren's world there is no hope of an afterlife."[10] The specific images of the Cross are only part, however, of a larger pattern of images through which Algren explores the guilt-love-death theme in a world of which Sophie says, "It's just the way things would be if that Nifty Louie was God and Blind Pig was Jesus Christ."

The earliest significant symbol in this Cross complex is the roach which Frankie sees enjoying its comfort beneath the radiator in the jail cell. Later, finding it struggling for its life in the water bucket, Frankie momentarily assumes the role of savior; but, "recalling that he, too, had leaped, or fallen, between walls he could not scale," he refuses to save the insect from the water until he himself is released from jail. When Frankie is bailed out after a short time, he looks into the bucket to save the roach but finds it dead. With prophetic remorse, he realizes that he could have saved a fellow creature from suffering, and thinks, "It's all my fault again." The futile struggle, the interdependence, the guilt, and the inescapable defeat of all major figures in the story are symbolized by the roach and by Frankie's role as the failing savior.

Other symbols in this complicated system of Christian images support and amplify its implications: the jailbirds wash as though they are taking baptism; Frankie returns to an apartment where a luminous crucifix is a constant accuser; after the New Year's party, the Division-Street Tower looks to Frankie like "a caricature of a Christmas tree"; during his jail term Frankie always kneels under a portrayal of the Station of the Cross labeled *Jesus Falls the First Time;* and Sophie feels that her wheelchair is her Cross and that she is nailed to it.

Captain Bednar and Sparrow the punk are also involved in explicit impalement images. At the moment Sparrow realizes that there is "no sort of living left in the alleys" whose sounds he hears "as familiarly as a nature lover hears murmurs of a forest morning," he sees a red kite caught like a bleeding cross on a telephone wire; and he feels "as if he too were something impaled on city wires for only tenement winds to touch." Too, as Bluestone has noted, Captain Bednar's "role as judge and sufferer is underlined in terms of crucifixion."[11]

VIII   *The Narcotics Angle: A Fortuitous Afterthought*

Though Algren's first version of his story contained nothing about drug addiction,[12] his integration of that material gave the novel wider impact than any other aspect of the tale. Though he asked his agent whether the narcotics angle might not be too sensational, he could hardly have foreseen that some readers would eventually regard *The Man with the Golden Arm* as primarily a "story about dope addiction" or that the movie industry would base a film version almost exclusively upon the tortures of withdrawal symptoms. Moreover, it is not likely that he could have guessed the success and even the notoriety he was to gain as a writer knowledgeable about a world of which little was known outside the closed groups of participants. Algren, unaware at first that he was associating with a group of addicts, became, in time, "very close to the drug scene" and in an advantageous position to follow his own precept: "if you listen long enough, the commonest speech will ring like poetry."[13]

Algren listened, as always. One result was that he extended almost to its limit his capacity for using the specialized street-and-alley jargon which gives his work both its poetic quality and its ring of authenticity. The world of the dope addict is also the jail-haunted world of "mush workers and lush workers, catamites and sodomites, bucket workers and bail jumpers, till tappers and assistant pickpockets, square Johns and copper Johns; lamisters and hallroom boys, ancient pious perverts and old blown parolees, rapoes and recordmen; the damned and the undaunted, the jaunty and condemned" who scratch on the walls of cramped cells the endless complaints and the "threadbare variations on the same age-old warnings against all the well-tried ancestral foes."

These catalogues of signatures, insignia, graffiti, confessions, admonitions, and borderline balladry constitute the great central registry of the city's twilight people. By this time, Algren was able to reconstruct the past civilizations of cell dwellers through their own forms of expression; to re-create the consuming, wary, nightly ritual of the professional poker game through its own incantatory tongue; and to record the quintessence of the junkies' mode of thought through their secret language.

The junkie's measure of the weight of his habit by the size of the "monkey on his back" gave Algren a phrase which found its way into common American usage. Algren says that, so far as he knows, the phrase was unknown except in the drug culture before the appearance of *The Man with the Golden Arm*. The monkey, which becomes one of the most effective motifs in the story, appears very early on the back of Private McGantic, who "stood stoop-shouldered by his terrible burden." The same imaginative projection, one which forces Frankie to identify himself with a condemned murderer until "in his mind Little Lester and himself had merged," makes Frankie think of himself as the monkey-ridden Private McGantic or, as he calls him in moments of wry bitterness, "Frantic McGantic." Indeed, as a form of alter-ego, McGantic becomes essential to Frankie's psychological defenses. When overwhelmed by the despair of his dependence upon Morphine, he could think and speak of himself only as the semi-objective alter-figure of McGantic; and he was able to feel "no pity for himself, yet felt compassion for this McGantic."

The ebb and flow of Frankie's war against morphine is traced in terms of the size of the monkey on his back. While patiently feeding Frankie's monkey, Louie "the Fixer" Fomorowsky, who has himself "gone from monkey to zero," assures Frankie that he hopes he, too, can starve the monkey to death; but Louie knows with the smug assurance of the seasoned fixer that the odds are at least ten thousand to one against any junkie's keeping the monkey-skeleton permanently unfleshed. In jail Frankie also succeeds in reducing his monkey to zero; but, home again and faced with the guilt for which he is punishing himself, he resumes his habit, soon fattening the monkey to the hypothetical thirty-five pounds which are more than any man can carry for long. It is true, as he has known all the time, that "the monkey never dies. When you kick him off, he just hops onto somebody else's back." Finally on Frankie's back again and growing heavier every hour, the grinning monkey rides him to death in a noose made of old-newspaper twine in a flophouse.

The dramatic and dreadful figure of the monkey is only one manifestation of Algren's thorough exploration of the drug addict's private world. With an understanding of the junkie's rationale which is amazing in one who has not himself been an addict, Algren brings to life not only the illusory assurances but also the failings, yearnings, and tortures of the narcotics addict. The process of addiction, by its very nature self-deceptive, is traceable only by the "fixer" who regards himself as a teacher. Therefore, like Bruno Bicek's graduation from vandalism to hoodlumhood, Frankie graduates from student to junkie; and Nifty Louie's increasing fixes are his certificates of progress. Frankie assures himself each time that he can survive without morphine and that each fix is his last, but he is aware of the truth in Louie's warning: "The way it starts is like this, students: you let the habit feed you first 'n one morning you wake up 'n you're feeding the habit."

Meantime, Frankie goes regularly and desperately to the "junkies' room" to renew the preserver-destroyer ceremony necessary to his life. In these scenes Algren creates a special kind of horror which lingers in readers' minds; and the description of the "junkies' room" itself is illustrative. It is the very epicenter of the junkie's daily consciousness, where the clock "told only Junkie Time. For every hour here was Old Junkies' Hour and the walls were the color of all old junkies' dreams: the hue of diluted morphine in the moment before the needle draws the suffering blood." Here, only one among a haunted procession of brief guests, Frankie Machine comes with "his life down to a tight pin point and the pupils of his eyes drawn even tighter: nothing is reflected in them except a capsule of light the size of a single quarter grain of morphine."

As Frankie falls upon the army cot beside the stove, he is in the torture of the junkie deprived beyond endurance: "The pain had hit him with an icy fist in the groin's very pit, momentarily tapering off to a single probing finger touching the genitals to get the maximum of pain. He tried twisting to get away from the finger: the finger was worse than the fist. His throat was so dry that, though he spoke, the lips moved and made no sound." During the interminable ritual of preparing the mixture, the sufferer cries "Hit me"; but the Fixer prolongs the agony with deliberate leisure. Knowing his business well, he is waiting with singular pleasure to watch the effects of the *whan* when "the big drive hits 'n here they come out of it cryin' like a baby 'r laughin' like a loon . . . you got to get the M to get that tingle-tingle."

The Man with the Golden Arm is, in fact, an encyclopedia of esoteric information about the usage and effects of various forms of drugs. One finds for instance, a piece of advice supplied by jailbird Applejack Katz:

"I've seen 'em hittin' C [cocaine], I've seen 'em hittin' M [morphine], I've seen 'em hittin' the H [heroin] 'n I've seen 'em shootin' speedballs — half a cap of C 'n half a cap of H together. C is the fastest, it's what they start on when they're after a gentleman's kick. M is slower 'n H is the slowest 'n cheapest of all, it's what they wind up on when they're just bummies tryin' to knock theirselves out with no kick at all. But I'll tell you one kick to lay off 'n that's nembutal. If you miss the vein you get an abscess 'n the shade comes down.

Or one sees the disgust of Sparrow the punk when he finds that Frankie smells *green* when he needs a fix badly. Or one learns the results of trying to kick the habit by tapering off with doses of codeine: the skin is too sensitive for the touch of water, the undeniable compulsion is to straighten things hanging crooked, and panic is created by a swinging light bulb.

For a reading public to whom, in the 1950's, the truly private world of the drug addict was remote but of intense interest, *The Man with the Golden Arm* was both an education and an emotional bombshell.

IX Structure: Unconventional Fusion

The three-stage development in the writing of *The Man with the Golden Arm* created what Bluestone has called "the novel's special aura."[14] The impact of the drug angle was due not so much to the sensational nature of the subject as to the fact that Algren had already constructed an engaging and meaningful story in which the narcotics problem could be made to play its part. The real power of the story lies in its extension and amplification of the "neighborhood novel" materials which Algren had explored successfully in *Never Come Morning*. Bluestone feels that the true center "lies in the complex relationship between Frankie and Sophie on the one hand, and between Frankie and Molly on the other."[15] To Maxwell Geismar, "the most telling success of the novel is the way Algren conveys the special quality of its feeling."[16]

Because the novel had grown in three stages, however, with shifts or additions of material at each stage, the integration of fresh material and the maintenance of steady focus became especially difficult problems. The result was an unconventional structure which has disturbed some critics. Looking back at *The Man with the Golden Arm* while commenting upon *A Walk on the Wild Side*, Norman Podhoretz decided that the earlier story was "full of half-realized attitudes identifying themselves only in a distant whisper; it was a book that never quite decided what it wanted to say," as contrasted with the later book, in which "there are no whispered intimations; the shouts are loud and clamorous enough for all to hear."[17] To most, however, the intimations seemed clear enough; and the overall structure seemed sufficiently obvious. They saw that the tale is constructed in two broad sections: the first, called "Rumors of Evening," in which Frankie struggles to overcome his feelings of guilt toward Sophie and to fend off his growing dependence upon morphine; the second, called "Act of Contrition," in which Frankie tries futilely to confront his failures and to purge himself of them through Molly's love.

Though little question has been raised about this general framework, Algren's method of fusing his materials within the broad pattern has aroused speculation. Algren himself has expressed some dissatisfaction with what he feels might be a somewhat over-obvious use of the near-melodramatic, near-cliché of the escape-pursuit motif. When asked what he would change, if anything, he replied: "I would avoid its cowboy-and-Indian ending. No gunfire and no big scenes. There is tragedy in America more common than a man being shot down in the street, more terrible than any police trap. It is the American disease of isolation, one which affects Americans from penthouse to tenement."[18]

Algren has said many times that he does not "plot" in the conventional sense. Looking back upon the creation of this novel, he has tried to envision in some detail the process he normally pursued: "I would start from that point where one man said, 'You don't know what it's like to have a thirty-pound monkey on your back — and you can go from there. Whether it's raining out, and where he's going, and what his name is, and what his story is. Proceeding from that, from the sense of anguish that he expresses in that phrase, I would think where else he could go and what else he might say."

Algren typically began such a story, therefore, by moving outward from a particularized sense of anguish. This method has led to the speculation that in such a tale as *The Man with the Golden Arm* "he is not primarily interested in either plot or idea"[19] but in mood. To charges that this story is sustained by tone and atmosphere at the expense of theme and structure, however, Bluestone answers that the appearance of disjointedness is purposeful. He believes it is the only appropriate scheme for a narrative which seeks to alternate a series of still-life pictures with the changes in consciousness which follow states of love or the destruction of love. "To reject Algren's structure is to reject his central vision,"[20] says Bluestone.

X *Assessment*

The Man with the Golden Arm is an estimable novel which occupies an important position in Algren's development as a novelist. Though not so neatly constructed as *Never Come Morning*, it is more densely packed, more intense, and in some ways more mature. The humorous scenes lead straight to Algren's last major work, the uniquely comic *A Walk on the Wild Side*, which Algren and many of his critics consider to be his best novel.

Like all important writers, Algren has been asked repeatedly to define the writer's role in modern society. He has struggled seriously to express the function he has sought to perform as a writer; and, though he has said it in many different ways, the gist is much the same: "The role of the writer is always to stand against the culture he is in,"[21] or more specifically, "the writer's place today is with the accused, guilty or not guilty, with the accused."[22]

The Man with the Golden Arm is Algren's most comprehensive expression of his conviction that America's great middle class should be made to recognize the personal worth and dignity of the socially disinherited who do not live the spurious lives of the "business cats" and the country-club set, neither of whom has been willing to recognize "the world underneath."[23] In writing such novels as *The Man with the Golden Arm*, Algren has blended Naturalistic Determinism "with a sympathy for his people that nevertheless cannot deter him from sending them to their miserable fates."[24] In a style and language that are drawn directly from the world he depicts, he has "managed to impart a dignity to material which would be merely sordid in the hands of a lesser writer."[25] He regularly insists that the "poetry" which characterizes his Realism is a natural poetry, one taken from the people themselves: "When I heard a convict who had just finished a stretch say, 'I made my time from bell to bell, now the rest of the way is by the stars,' if somebody was fusing poetry with realism it was the con, not me. My most successful poetry, the lines people threw back at me years after they were written, were lines I never wrote. They were lines I heard, and repeated, usually by someone who never read and couldn't write."[26]

For this reason, despite the concreteness and authoritative detail of his prose, Algren is "more a singer than an explainer,"[27] one whose prose in *The Man with the Golden Arm* can become almost a "kind of incantation, like the chanting of ritual itself."[28] In such a form, the curb and tenement and half-shadow world of Frankie and Sophie and Molly with its unforgettable smoke-colored rain, its musk-colored murmuring, and its calamitous light have brought the world underneath a bit closer to the middle-class American consciousness and conscience.

CHAPTER 6

Poet and Prophet

NELSON Algren now calls himself a journalist, which he, of course, is and has been since he was graduated from the University of Illinois in 1931. Nevertheless, his four novels, his some fifty short stories, his numerous sketches, essays, poetry, prose poems, travel books, book reviews, and other literary criticism produced during nearly four decades of writing assure him a place in American literature. Indeed, recognition, in the form of the first National Book Award and grants from the American Academy of Arts and Letters and the Newberry Library, has been accorded his work.

His last two novels also gained sufficient public acceptance to appear for several months on best-seller lists, and both were dramatized for stage productions and made into Hollywood movies. His collection of short stories *The Neon Wilderness*, has been highly praised: Maxwell Geismar calls it "an excellent collection of short stories, perhaps one of the best we had in the 1940's."[1] *The Man with the Golden Arm* was awarded the National Book Award as 1949's most distinguished American novel; and Blanche Gelfant considers it "the outstanding city novel" of the decade.[2] *A Walk on the Wild Side*, Algren's favorite work as well as that of most of his latest critics, is acclaimed for its prophetic qualities and for its influence on other novelists

Algren's overall influence is hard to assess at this time. His popular appeal has never again reached the height it attained with the success of *The Man with the Golden Arm* in 1949, and his last major fictional work, *A Walk on the Wild Side*, was published in 1956. Some critics have complained that he has wasted his time since then on less significant projects like travel books, which seem to them unworthy of his talents and far below the stature of his earlier achievements. Yet some loyal followers have noted an increase in Algren's control and mastery of style, mood, comic sense, and message in some of the later stories and sketches.

His book shelves are filled with the work of fellow novelists, many of whom acknowledge in their inscriptions his importance in literature and their personal debt to him. Two of these inscriptions, ones separated by almost two decades, suffice to illustrate. A first edition of Wright's *Native Son,* published in 1940, is inscribed:

> To —
>   My old friend
>   Nelson
> Who I believe is still
> the best writer of good
> prose in the U.S.A.
>   Dick

Almost three decades later, George Bluestone, perhaps Algren's most perceptive critic, wrote on the flyleaf of a copy of his own novel, *The Send-Off:*

>   January, 1969
>   To Nelson —
>   who showed
>   us all the
>   way . . .
>   George

Critics have frequently commented that much of Algren's work was ahead of its time. Two decades before drug addiction became a national dilemma, *The Man with the Golden Arm* fictionized the world of the drug addict with authority and impact as yet unsurpassed. Algren once said that no one has ever understood *A Walk on the Wild Side,* for it is a book of a kind never before written, "an American fantasy — a poem written to an American beat as truly as *Huckleberry Finn.*"[3] This "parody of the young man on the make for money and success"[4] proved Algren to be prophet as well as poet, for that book is a precursor of the much later novel (and film) *Midnight Cowboy* by James L. Herlihy, and of the film *Easy Rider;* and an admitted influence exists on the first if not on the latter. Ralph J. Gleason commented most recently and succinctly on the influence of Nelson Algren, particularly of his last novel:

A *Walk on the Wild Side* is available in paperback and it deserves to be read by every *Catch 22* and *Cuckoo's Nest* freak just so they can find out what opened the door for two novels that had the same kind of effect on the changing American consciousness that Bob Dylan has had. It's not only that before Heller and Kesey there was Algren. It's that Algren is where they came from, and the fantasy/reality, inside/outside paradoxical view of the inversion of the American Dream that is central to their books was first laid out by Algren in A *Walk on the Wild Side*.[5]

Gleason, noting that quotations from Algren's books are seen everywhere today, predicts that he is " 'bubbling under' as they say in the Billboard chart" and is "about to get out there again like Bessie Smith, a late-blooming hit parader." Though Bob Dylan may never have read A *Walk on the Wild Side*, Gleason says, he nevertheless set it to music; and Gleason also comments about Algren's effect on other writers: "Up until Algren, no American writer had really combined a poetic gift for words and a vision of the truth about the textbook democracy. He saw it gradually or all at once it makes no difference, and he put it down in the one novel which blew the minds of hundreds of other writers. . . ."[6]

When an interviewer asked Algren about evidence of specific borrowings from his work, particularly that of the legless man, who has, since Algren created him, appeared in the work of several others, Algren replied:

No proprietary rights over amputees. Captain Ahab and Porgy were around before Railroad Shorty rolled on. If you explore new country cautious men will follow. Once I reported a kid who, when sentenced to the electric chair, said, "I knew I'd never get to be twenty-one anyhow." That was before the war. When I got out, the kid had gone to work for a neighboring novelist. I started going to the police line-ups. A couple of pieces in *Esquire* and they were adapted for radio and later for TV. Why not? The neighboring novelist used them fairly effectively. I went out and brought back the man with the thirty-five-pound monkey on his back. Again he showed up with the N.N. I began hoping N.N. wouldn't snatch Railroad Shorty. Just then I heard the thunder of little wheels, and sure enough — here comes Railroad Shorty. The N.N. didn't know what to do with him, he just wanted to have an amputee too.[7]

Algren recently wrote that he perceives only now that the Freudian key to everything he has written lies in one of the lyrics he composed for Schmidt, the legless man on the platform in A *Walk on the Wild Side*. The lyric, "The Room with the Low-Knobbed Door," is one of two Algren wrote for Schmidt to sing in the musical version of the novel presented at the Crystal Palace in St. Louis in 1960. Though the lyric has remained unpublished, Algren has granted permission for its inclusion here:

The Room with the Low-Knobbed Door

Here in the room with the low-knobbed door
Where the years like wheels have rolled me
Iron years like iron wheels
When forty of them rolled o'er me
When the sky holds a kind of criminal glow
Full of longing and full of loss
And the whiskey in the glass before you
Is one whiskey you won't toss

Then is that Tell-Me-All-About-It
That Let-Me-Talk-To-You-Mister Hour
That Twenty-Cents-Will-See-Me-Through
That All-Night Pleader's Hour.
I hear the two-leggers hurrying
To Home, to love and to rest
As none has my envy, none has my love
And a wind off the flat ice-plains of death
Blows under the low-knobbed door.

So long past four. So long till day.
The Birmingham Grizzly — that was me.
Though the girls all called me The Honeyfed Bear
There was always confetti and always applause
When The Honeyfed Bear showed his terrible claws
And no man in my circuit broke my lock
And no man put me down.

So long past five so long till six
And though death himself find my lonesome stair
And trap me unstrapped and naked here
He'll draw short breath and work up a sweat
He'll need a lock stronger than my own
Before he pulls me down.

Well, a man on wheels is a kind of a clown
(You can tell when the two-legger smiles down)
But that's all in the game, it's all in a day

Take the bitter along with the sweet I say
And I'll give any man the same square play
The Santa Fe wheels gave me.

Now the last of the two-leggers hurrying home
Leaves me and my small steel wheels alone
Yet none have my mercy as none have my love
I ask mercy of no man, pity of none
But e'er the last of the lights go out
In some hour of the outcast and unused whore
God, make me one great claw.

Now here comes daybreak steadily
Down the long uncarpeted hall
One off at the hip and one at the knee
Kneewalking to a low-knobbed door.

As Maxwell Geismar has noted, Algren belongs to a literary tradition of social protest which is to a degree unfashionable in fiction today. But, as Geismar concludes, though Algren must at times feel
isolated, "he also represents a solid and enduring part of the
American heritage of dissent" and he "should take comfort from the
past, even while he writes, as all artists do, for the future; and, in his
own words, he is still in there, 'toughing it out!' "[8]

Since 1956, Algren has not attempted another major novel. For
some time, he has considered material for a book which, tentatively,
he would call *Entrapment*. Over a period of years he has also worked
on a "racetrack novel"; and portions of it — "The Moon of the Arfy
Darfy,"[9] "A Ticket on Skoronski,"[10] and "Get All the Money"[11] —
have been published separately. But, despite the urging of friends,
he feels no temptation to do another "big book": "I'm not willing to
knock myself out on a 'big book' only to have it degraded by one
Preminger or another. What for? I live in a city which is the capital
of the Silent Majority and I don't intend to knock myself out against
the wall of that silence. I get by well enough between junkets to
Europe and Southeast Asia, on short story writing, platform
appearances, and betting on horses."

Algren lived in Saigon from December to May of 1968-1969, and
he has written a number of articles on his observations and experiences there. Some are included in a book of essays, sketches, and
short stories which, under the title *The Last Carousel*, was published
late in 1973, as the manuscript for this study was going to press.

When Algren is not traveling, he occupies his flat on the third and top story of a comfortable but unimposing apartment house in what he calls a "quiet neighborhood" near the intersection of Damen and Division Streets, the center of *The Man with the Golden Arm* locale. There, in a comfortable clutter, surrounded by walls lined from top to bottom with pictures, photographs, artifacts, and mementos of his travels and friendships, sidestepping piles of books that have overflowed from his book cases, he belabors his two favorite typewriters.

He still turns persistently to poetry, which he enjoys both writing and reading aloud. Still faithful, in his fashion, to a Chicago in which various neighborhoods are disappearing under the impact of urban housing developments, he is alert to changes in society, politics, economics, sports, and the arts. He keeps in touch with a limited circle of friends, most regularly with Stephen Deutch, a sculptor and photographer. He enjoys taking friends to the many excellent but often obscure restaurants which have survived urban renewal, including a good Italian place whose cook once worked for Al Capone. Wherever Algren is known, he commands an easy-going but unmistakable respect; and up and down Division Street in sporadic sections where something of the old neighborhood survives, he can still be at home among the stumblebums whose bard he has become.

Whether or not Algren writes another novel, his position as "one of the shapers of contemporary literature" seems secure. He is, as J. W. Corrington asserts, one of the few "American" as opposed to Southern, Jewish, New Yorker, or San Francisco writers around today. And he is still "alive and talking."[12]

Notes and References

Chapter One

1. Maxwell Geismar, "Nelson Algren: The Iron Sanctuary," *English Journal*, XLII (March, 1953): 124.
2. Malcolm Cowley, "Chicago Poem," *New Republic*, CVI, Part 2 (May 4, 1942): 614.
3. Leslie Fiedler, "The Noble Savages of Skid Row," *The Reporter*, XV (July 12, 1956): 44.
4. *Ibid.*, p. 43.
5. Algren, quoted by H. E. F. Donohue, *Conversations With Nelson Algren* (New York: Hill and Wang, 1964), p. 10. Hereafter referred to as Donohue.
6. *Ibid.*, p. 6.
7. From taped interviews between Algren and the authors of this study. The first series of interviews took place in Algren's apartment in Chicago from August 26-28, 1969. Subsequent visits, letters, and telephone conversations for the next four years, including a one-hour taped telelecture to Martha Cox's "Seminar in Southern Fiction" at San Jose State University, provided additional information. Hereafter, unfootnoted quotations and information about either Algren or his work not attributed to others are from our own interviews and correspondence.
8. Donohue, *op. cit.*, p. 28.
9. *Somebody in Boots*, Berkeley Medallion Edition (New York, 1965), p. 141.
10. Donohue, *op. cit.*, p. 52.
11. Kenneth Allsop, "Talk on the Wild Side," *Spectator*, CCIII (October 16, 1959): 509.
12. Philip Rahv, "No Parole," *Nation*, CLIV (April 18, 1942): 466.
13. Benjamin Appel, *Saturday Review of Literature*, XXV (April 18, 1942): 7.
14. "I Ain't Abelard," *Newsweek*, LXIV (December 28, 1964): 58.
15. "The Question of Simone de Beauvoir," *Harper's*, CCXXX (May, 1965): 136.

16. Fiedler, "The Noble Savages of Skid Row," 43.

17. David Ray, "A Talk on the Wild Side; A Bowl of Coffee with Nelson Algren" (interview), *The Reporter*, XX (June 11, 1959): 32.

18. S. P. M., *Saturday Review*, XXXIX (May 26, 1956): 16.

19. Correspondence with authors, September, 1970. See note 7.

20. "Hollywood Djinn," *Nation*, CLXXVII (July 25, 1953): 68-70.

21. Budd Schulberg, "Heartbeat of a City," *New York Times Book Review* (October 21, 1951): 3.

22. Harry Hansen, "Fighting Hymn to Chicago," *New York Herald Tribune Book Review* (October 21, 1951): 15.

23. Fiedler, "The Noble Savages of Skid Row," 43.

24. Norman Podhoretz, "The Man With the Golden Beef," *New Yorker*, XXXII (June 2, 1956): 126.

25. Lawrence Lipton, "A Voyeur's View of the Wild Side: Nelson Algren and His Reviewers," *Chicago Review*, X, 4 (Winter, 1957): 37-39.

26. James T. Farrell, "On the Wrong Side of Town," *New Republic*, CXXXIV (May 21, 1956): 18.

27. David Ray's interview with Algren, "A Talk on the Wild Side," 31. Algren reaffirmed this point of view in our interviews.

28. Herbert Gold, "After All, Who Is the Enemy?" *New York Times Book Review* (June 2, 1963): 23.

29. Norman Mailer, "The Big Bite," *Esquire*, LX (September, 1963): 16-21.

30. William Barrett, "Citizens of the World," *Atlantic Monthly*, CXI (June, 1963): 132-133.

31. Hilton Kramer, "He Never Left Home," *The Reporter*, XXVIII (June 20, 1963): 46-47.

32. "Un-American Notes," *The Times (London) Literary Supplement* (January 9, 1964): 32.

33. "Baedeker with a Bite," *Newsweek*, LXI (May 13, 1963): 108.

34. "Intellectual as Ape Man," *Time*, LXXXI (May 31, 1963): 84-85.

35. See Morley Callaghan, "Legends of the Old Man," *Saturday Review*, XLVIII (August 28, 1965): 43.

36. Edward Weeks, "Algren: Afire and Afloat," *Atlantic Monthly*, XXXVI (August, 1965): 122.

37. Sol Yurick, "Correspondent to the Underworld," *Nation*, CCI (October 25, 1965): 283.

38. "The Wildest Side," *Newsweek*, LXVI (August 16, 1965): 82.

39. Arno Karlen, *New York Times Book Review*, (August 22, 1965): 4.

40. C. H. Simonds, "Books in Brief," *National Review*, XVII (September 21, 1965): 840.

41. Callaghan, *op. cit.*, p. 43.

42. John Leonard, "Monsters, Butter-Pastry, Saltines," *National Review*, XV (December 31, 1963): 571.

43. John Barkham, "The Fellow Had the Tape, And Algren Liked to Talk," *This World, San Francisco Sunday Chronicle*, November 8, 1964, p.

40. This article is typical of the attitude of these critics.

Chapter Two

1. Alston Anderson and Terry Southern (interview), "Nelson Algren," *Writers at Work; The Paris Review Interviews* (New York: The Viking Press, 1958), p. 240.

2. Charles Child Walcutt, *American Literary Naturalism: A Divided Stream* (Minneapolis, 1956), p. 69.

3. George Bluestone, "Nelson Algren," *Western Review*, XXII (Autumn, 1957): 35.

4. For a full-length study of this aspect of Algren's work, see the unpublished dissertation (University of Iowa, 1967) of Robert Edwin Omick, "Compassion in the Novels of Nelson Algren."

5. See Edwin M. Moseley, *Pseudonyms of Christ in the Modern Novel* (Pittsburgh, 1962).

6. Bluestone, *op. cit.*, p. 33.

7. Chester E. Eisinger, "Nelson Algren: Naturalism as the Beat of the Iron Heart," *Fiction of the Forties* (Chicago, 1963), p. 81.

8. See pp. 63-64.

9. The version of the story which appeared in *American Mercury*, LXIV (January, 1947): 26-35, is somewhat different from the version in *The Neon Wilderness*. Just before the fight, Fancy's eye falls upon a cash register sign saying CASH PURCHASE instead of NO CREDIT, and the NO SALE sign is not used.

10. Bluestone, *op. cit.*, p. 35.

11. "Chicago without Tears or Dreams" (review of *Neon Wilderness*), *Saturday Review of Literature*, XXX (February 8, 1947): 14.

12. Geismar, "Nelson Algren: The Iron Sanctuary," p. 123.

13. *Ibid.*, p. 123.

Chapter Three

1. For valuable distinctions among these terms, see Frederick Feied, *No Pie in the Sky; The Hobo as American Cultural Hero in the Works of Jack London, John Dos Passos, and Jack Kerouac* (New York, 1964).

2. Eisinger, *op. cit.*, p. 77.

3. Geismar, "Nelson Algren: The Iron Sanctuary," p. 122.

4. Geismar, "Algren Weaves 'Wild, Wonderful' Tale," *Chicago Sun Times*, May 20, 1956, section 2, p. 4. Here, Geismar remarked, "The difference between these books is the real measure of the writer's development."

5. Bluestone, "Nelson Algren," p. 40.

6. Algren provided this information in a telelecture interview with Martha Cox's "Seminar in Southern Fiction" at San Jose State University, May 15, 1970. The interview was taped. See note 7, Chapter I.

7. David Ray, "A Talk on the Wild Side; A Bowl of Coffee with Nelson Algren" (interview), *The Reporter*, XX (June 11, 1959): 32.

8. Though Algren is not generally known as a practitioner of this kind of linguistic symbolism, it is interesting to note the irony in a literal translation of this name from the Spanish: "the little Teresa of the varied life." In connection with Algren's choice of names, this passage from our interviews is revealing: "I like to see a name up somewhere. You know, you like to see a name on a store front or something . . . . Dove, Dovey — I was looking at some coroner's inquests, and there was a Negro woman's inquest, her name was Dovey Breedlove — so I got Dove out of that. And I just wanted a Southern name, you know, and they call guys Marion down there, and Irene, so I called this guy Dove."

9. Norman Podhoretz, "The Man with the Golden Beef," *New Yorker*, XXXII (June 2, 1956): 126.

10. Maxwell Geismar, "Against the Tide of Euphoria," *Nation*, CXXXII (June 2, 1956): 473.

11. Max Baird, "Powerful New Novel," *Columbia Missourian*, May 22, 1956.

12. From an unpublished letter William Peden, University of Missouri, wrote to Algren's publisher. The letter, which was forwarded to Algren, is now in his scrapbooks.

13. Luther Nichols, "Digging Deep into the Underworld," *San Francisco Examiner*, May 20, 1956.

14. Ralph Blagden, "Algren's Shocking World of Half Men Holds Some Hope," *Sacramento Bee*, June 8, 1956.

15. Milton Rugoff, "An Exuberant Novel of the Lower Depths," *New York Herald Tribune*, May 20, 1956, p. 4.

16. Bluestone, *op. cit.*, p. 41.

17. Jennie Puryear Gardner, "Compassion for Derelicts," *Louisville Courier-Journal*, May 20, 1956.

18. Because Hallie's Negro blood had cost her a career as a schoolteacher, it is worthwhile to note that in our interviews Algren said, "Breedlove is a very common Negro name."

19. Podhoretz, *op. cit.*, p. 126.

20. Anderson and Southern, *op. cit.*, p. 244.

21. Alfred Kazin, "Some People Passing By," *New York Times Book Review*, May, 1956.

22. "Rough Stuff," *Time*, LXVII (May 28, 1956): 106.

23. Martha Smith, "Enchanted Windows," *The Hartsdale* (New York) *News*, May 24, 1956.

24. William Root, "The Depraved — Are They Really the Best People?" *People Today*, June 29, 1956.

25. Leslie A. Fiedler, "The Noble Savages of Skid Row," *The Reporter*, XV (July 12, 1956): 43.

26. "Plumbing the Depths," *Newsweek* (July 2, 1956): 74.

27. Lipton, *op. cit.*, p. 39.

28. Jennie Puryear Gardner, *op. cit.*

29. Rugoff, *op. cit.*, p. 4.

30. John D. Weaver, "Algren Has Talk on the Wild Side," *Independent Star-News*, June 3, 1956.

31. Harnett T. Kane, "Corrosive Comment," *The Houston Post*, June 10, 1956.

32. James Kelly, "Sin-Soaked in Storyville," *Saturday Review*, XXXIX (May 26, 1956): 16.

33. Kenneth C. Crabbe, "Author of 'Golden Arm' Returns to His Derelicts," *Augusta Chronicle-Herald*, July 22, 1956.

34. Ray, *op. cit.*, p. 33.

35. *Movies on TV* (New York, Bantam Books, Inc., 1936), p. 372.

36. John William Corrington, "Nelson Algren Talks with NOR's Editor-at-Large," *The New Orleans Review*, I (Winter, 1969): 131.

37. *A Walk on the Wild Side* was often reviewed simultaneously with *The World of Suzie Wong*, a popular "brothel novel" by Richard Mason, published at about the same time. But Mason's novel was directly in the tradition of the good-hearted whore, and the superiority of Algren's novel is attested to by evidence that Mason's book is virtually forgotten today.

38. Lipton, "A Voyeur's View of the Wild Side," p. 34. See also some remarks on the other side of the question: Luise Putcamp, Jr., "Middlebrow's Bookshelf," *Ogden* (Utah) *Standard-Examiner*, July 8, 1956; and "Rough Stuff," *Time*, LXVII (May 28, 1956: 106.

39. Kelly, *op. cit.*, p. 16.

40. "Algren, Miller, Fisher Make a Turbulent Trio," *Dallas Morning News*, July 8, 1956.

41. Nichols, *op. cit.*

42. Baird, *op. cit.*

43. Van Allen Bradley, "Algren's Latest Novel Rich in Word Imagery," *Chicago Daily News* (undated clipping in Algren's scrapbook).

44. Ralph J. Gleason, "Perspectives: Is It Out of Control?" *Rolling Stone*, (August 6, 1970): 9.

Chapter Four

1. Cowley, *op. cit.*, p. 613.

2. Interview. See note 7, Chapter 1.

3. Nelson Algren, "Remembering Richard Wright," *Nation*, CXCII (January 28, 1961): 85.

4. Geismar, "Nelson Algren: The Iron Sanctuary," p. 122.

5. Bluestone, "Nelson Algren," p. 31.

6. Eisinger, *op. cit.*, p. 77.

7. Bruno's image of himself at these moments appears to be simply that of the wolf as a lone prowler, not in the slang sense of "wolf" as one who is

intent upon pursuing women, nor in the Existential sense involving the abstractions of Hermann Hesse's *Steppenwolf.*

8. The young people in this novel habitually use Polish words for common American terms: *gospoda* is *tavern* or *saloon; gotówka* is spending money or ready cash; *Apteka* is a *drug store.*

9. Eisinger, *op. cit.,* p. 79.

10. Cowley, *op. cit.,* p. 613.

11. Bluestone, *op. cit.,* p. 31.

12. Cowley, *op. cit.,* p. 613.

13. Fiedler, "The Noble Savages of Skid Row," 43.

14. Philip Rahv, "No Parole," *Nation,* CLIV (April 18, 1942): 466.

15. Harry Hansen, "The First Reader," *New York World-Telegram* (April 16, 1942).

16. Bluestone, *op. cit.,* p. 32.

17. Lipton, *op. cit.,* p. 35.

18. Eisinger, *op. cit.,* p. 83.

19. *Ibid.,* p. 80.

20. Bluestone, *op. cit.,* p. 32.

21. *Ibid.,* p. 33.

22. Some idea of Algren's eye for detail and his sense of the dramatic in prize-fighting tactics may be gained through the following anecdote: In a sedate cocktail lounge of the Palmer House in Chicago, while describing a championship heavyweight prize fight to the co-authors of this study, Algren stood beside the table and pantomimed a full sequence of actions leading to a knockout.

23. Rahv, *op. cit.,* p. 466.

24. Benjamin Appel, "People of Crime," *Saturday Review of Literature,* XXV (April 18, 1942): 7.

Chapter Five

1. From the Cox and Chatterton interviews.

2. Anderson and Southern, *op. cit.,* p. 235.

3. *Ibid.,* p. 236.

4. Les Brown, "Algren a Sociable Guy — Socially Conscious Writer," *Roosevelt Torch,* October 24, 1949, p. 5.

5. George Murray, "Author of 'The Man with the Golden Arm' Takes a Walk Amid His Old West Side Haunts," *Chicago American,* "Pictorial Living," October 7, 1956. The tavern was closed by the time the article was written.

6. Bluestone, *op. cit.,* p. 36.

7. Eisinger, *op. cit.,* p. 82.

8. Algren has a special fondness for cats. In autographing his books, he sometimes draws pictures of cats in various colors of crayon or colored pencil. He often concludes personal letters, too, with a cat drawing or, more recently, a replica of the Cookie Monster.

9. "Fellini's 'La Dolce Vita,' " a discussion by Nelson Algren, Mario de Vecchi, Studs Terkel, *wfmt Chicago Fine Arts Guide*, X, 8 (August, 1961): 9.

10. Bluestone, *op. cit.*, pp. 37-38.

11. *Ibid.*, p. 68.

12. An early prospectus of *The Man with the Golden Arm*, titled *The Chair*, contains no hint of the drug addiction material.

13. Algren, "Do It the Hard Way," *The Writer*, LVI (March, 1943): 69.

14. Bluestone, *op. cit.*, p. 36.

15. *Ibid.*

16. Eisinger, *op. cit.*, p. 82.

17. Norman Podhoretz, "The Man with the Golden Beef," *The New Yorker*, XXXII (June 2, 1956): 126.

18. Ray, *op. cit.*, p. 32.

19. Eisinger, *op cit.*, p. 82.

20. Bluestone, *op. cit.*, p. 39.

21. "The Role of the Writer in America," The 4th Literary Symposium Sponsored by *Esquire* Magazine at the University of Michigan, with Vance Bourjaily, William Styron, Nelson Algren, and Gore Vidal, 1961. In *Voices*, II, 3 (Spring, 1962).

22. Lipton, *op. cit.*, p. 41.

23. Bernard Gavzer, "Noted Author Insists Cheap Flat Suits Him Fine," *Bergen Evening Record*, August 18, 1950.

24. Eisinger, *op. cit.*, p. 84.

25. John J. Maloney, "Chicago: Seamy Side," *New York Herald Tribune*, September 11, 1949.

26. Luther Nichols, "An Author Explains His Views," *San Francisco Examiner*, May 20, 1956.

27. Eisinger, *op. cit.*, p. 82.

28. Bluestone, *op. cit.*, p. 38.

Chapter Six

1. Geismar, "Nelson Algren: The Iron Sanctuary," p. 123.

2. Blanche Gelfant, *The American City Novel*, Second Edition (Norman, 1970), p. 252.

3. Ray, *op. cit.*, p. 32.

4. Lipton, *op. cit.*, p. 34.

5. Ralph J. Gleason, "Perspectives: Is It Out of Control?" *Rolling Stone*, (August 6, 1970): 9.

6. *Ibid.*

7. Ray, *op. cit.*, p. 33.

8. Geismar, "Nelson Algren: The Iron Sanctuary," p. 125.

9. "The Moon of the Arfy Darfy," *Saturday Evening Post*, CCXXXVII (September 26, 1964): 44-45.

10. "A Ticket on Skoronski," *Saturday Evening Post*, CCXXXIX (November 5, 1966): 48-49.

11. "Get All the Money," *Playboy*, XVII (June, 1970): 82-84, 86, 98, 186-88, 191, 194.

12. "Nelson Algren Talks with NOR's Editor-at-Large," *The New Orleans Review*, I, 2 (Winter, 1969): 130.

Selected Bibliography

PRIMARY SOURCES

No attempt has been made to list foreign editions of Algren's works; book and film reviews and most newspaper articles are also omitted; and the short stories listed separately are only those which do not appear in *The Neon Wilderness*, or, unless they have been revised or retitled, in *The Last Carousel*.

1. Books

Chicago: City on the Make. New York: Doubleday, 1951.

Chicago: City on the Make. Sausalito, California: Contact Editions, 1961.

Chicago: City on the Make (new epilogue and twenty-four photographs by Stephen Deutch). Oakland, California: Angel Island Publications, Inc., 1968.

Chicago: City on the Make (limited edition of one hundred copies identical to the previous entry except for a different epilogue title). Oakland, California: Angel Island Publications, Inc., 1968.

Conversations with Nelson Algren (with H. E. F. Donohue). New York: Hill and Wang, 1964.

Conversations with Nelson Algren (with H. E. F. Donohue). New York: Berkeley Medallion Edition, 1965.

The Jungle (an adaptation of *Somebody in Boots*). New York: Avon Publications, Inc., undated.

The Last Carousel (a collection of stories and sketches, including "Dark Came Early in That Country," "Could World War I Have Been a Mistake?", "Otto Preminger's Strange Suspenjers," "I Never Hollered Cheezit the Cops," "The Mad Laundress of Dingdong-Daddyland," "The Leak That Defied the Books," "Tinkle Hinkle and the Footnote King," "Hand in Hand Through the Greenery with the grandstand clowns of arts and letters," "Come In If You Love Money," "Brave Bulls of Sidi Yahya," "I Know They'll Like Me in Saigon," "Airy Persiflage on the Heaving Deep," "No Cumshaw No Rickshaw," "Letter from Saigon," "What Country Do You Think You're In?",

"Police and Mama-sans Get It All," "Poor Girls of Kowloon," "After the Buffalo," "The Cortez Gang," "The House of the Hundred Grass-fires," "Previous Days," "Epitaph: *The Man with the Golden Arm*," "The Passion of Upside-Down-Emil: *A Story from Life's Other Side*," "Merry Christmas Mr. Mark," "I Guess You Fellows Just Don't Want Me," "Everything Inside Is a Penny," "The Ryebread Trees of Spring," "Different Clowns of Different Towns," "Go! Go! Go! Forty Years Ago," "Ballet for Opening Day: *The Swede Was a Hard Guy*," "A Ticket on Skoronski," "Ode to an Absconding Bookie," "Bullring of the Summer Night," "Moon of the Arfy Darfy," "Watch Out for Daddy," "The Last Carousel," and "Tricks Out of Times Long Gone"). New York: G. P. Putnam's Sons, 1973.

The Man with the Golden Arm. Garden City, New York: Doubleday, 1949. (The typescripts of the four versions of the novel, the galley proof, and the proof copy are in the collections of the Ohio State University Libraries.)

The Man with the Golden Arm. New York: Fawcett World Library, undated.

Nelson Algren's Own Book of Lonesome Monsters (a collection of short stories edited by Algren; Algren wrote the Preface and the concluding story "The House of the Hundred Grassfires"). New York: Lancer Books, Inc., 1962.

Nelson Algren's Own Book of Lonesome Monsters (with an added section of biographical notes entitled "The Authors"). New York: Bernard Geis Associates, 1963.

The Neon Wilderness (a collection of short stories, including "The Captain Has Bad Dreams," "How the Devil Came Down Division Street," "Is Your Name Joe?", "Depend on Aunt Elly," "Stickman's Laugh-ter," "A Bottle of Milk for Mother," "He Couldn't Boogie-woogie Worth a Damn," "A Lot You got to Holler," "Poor Man's Pennies," "The Face on the Barroom Floor," "The Brother's House," "Please Don't Talk about Me when I'm Gone," "He Swung and He Missed," "El Presidente de Mejico," "Kingdom City to Cairo," "That's the Way It's Always Been," "The Children," "Million-dollar Brainstorm," "Pero Venceremos," "No Man's Laughter," "Katz," "Design for De-parture," "The Heroes," and "So Help Me"). Garden City, New York: Doubleday, 1947.

The Neon Wilderness (with a new introduction by the author). New York: Hill and Wang, Inc., 1960.

Never Come Morning (with an introduction by Richard Wright). New York: Harper, 1942.

Never Come Morning (with a new Preface by the author). New York: Harper and Row, 1963.

Notes from a Sea Diary: Hemingway All the Way. New York: G. P. Putnam's Sons, 1965.

Notes from a Sea Diary: Hemingway All the Way. Greenwich, Conn.: Fawcett Publications, Inc., 1966.

Somebody in Boots. New York: Farrar, Straus and Giroux, 1935.

Somebody in Boots (with a new Preface by the author). New York: Berkeley Publishing Corporation, 1965.

A Walk on the Wild Side. New York: Farrar, Straus and Cudahy, 1956.

A Walk on the Wild Side. New York: Fawcett World Library, 1962.

Who Lost an American? New York: Macmillan, 1963.

2. Short Stories

"All Through the Night," *Playboy* IV (April, 1957): 29, 69-72. (Reprinted in *The Permanent Playboy*. New York: Crown Publishers, Inc., 1959. This piece also constitutes the middle section of "Watch Out for Daddy" in *The Last Carousel*.)

"Biceps," *Southern Review*, VI, 4 (1941); 713-28.

"Buffalo Sun," *The Calithump*, I (April, 1934); 13-14.

"The Captain Is Impaled," *Harper's Magazine*, CXCIX (August, 1949): 88-96. (Reprinted and retitled "The Mad Laundress of Dingdong-Daddyland" in *The Last Carousel*.)

"Decline and Fall of Dingdong-Daddyland," *Commentary* XLVIII (September, 1969): 69-76.

"Ding-ding, Tinkle Hinkle, The Finkified Lasagna and the Footnote King," *Dial*, I, no. 1 (Fall, 1959): 125-31. (Revised, reprinted, and retitled "Tinkle Hinkle and the Footnote King" in *The Last Carousel*.)

"The Donkeyman by Twilight," *Nation*, CXCVIII (May 18, 1964): 509-12.

"Down with All Hands," *Atlantic*, CCVI (December, 1960): 76-84.

"The Father and Son Cigar," *Playboy*, IX (December, 1962): 120-21, 186-88, 190, 192, 194. (Reprinted in *The Bedside Playboy*. Chicago: The Playboy Press, 1963, pp. 97-111. Reprinted and retitled "Everything Inside Is a Penny" in *The Last Carousel*.)

"Forgive them, Lord," *A Year Magazine*, (December, 1933-April, 1934): 144-49.

"Get All the Money," *Playboy*, XVII (June, 1970): 82-89, 98, 186-98. (Revised, reprinted, and retitled "Bullring of the Summer Night" in *The Last Carousel*.)

"God Bless the Lonesome Gas Man," *The Dude*, VI, 4 (March 1962): 11-12, 73. (Revised, reprinted, and retitled "The Leak that Defied the Books" in *The Last Carousel*.)

"Home to Shawneetown," *Atlantic Monthly*, CCXXII (August, 1968): 41-47. (Revised and retitled "Dark Came Early in that Country" in *The Last Carousel*.)

"The House of the Hundred Grassfires," *Nelson Algren's Own Book of Lonesome Monsters*. New York: Bernard Geis Associates, 1963, pp. 192-210. (Material deleted before publication from *A Walk on the Wild Side*; reprinted in *The Last Carousel*.)

"If You Must Use Profanity," *American Mercury*, XXXI (April, 1934): 430-36.

"Ipso Facto," *Audience*, I (November-December, 1971): 78-81. (Reprinted and retitled "I Guess You Fellas Just Don't Want Me" in *The Last Carousel*.)

"The Last Carousel," *Playboy*, XVIII (February, 1972): 72, 74, 76, 126, 180, 182-86, 188, 190. (Revised and reprinted in *The Last Carousel*.)

"A Lumpen," *The New Masses: Short Story Number*, XVI (July 2, 1935): 25-26.

"The Moon of the Arfy Darfy," *Saturday Evening Post*, CCXXXVII (September 26, 1964): 44-45. (Revised, reprinted, and retitled "Moon of the Arfy Darfy" in *The Last Carousel*.)

"The Peseta with the Hole in the Middle, Part I," (pre-print) *The Kenyon Review*, XXIII (Autumn, 1961): 549-70.

"The Peseta with the Hole in the Middle, Part II," *The Kenyon Review*, XXIV (Winter, 1962): 110-28.

"Single Exit," *Cross Section*. Edited by Edwin Seaver. New York: Simon and Schuster, 1947. pp. 217-24.

"Swan Lake Reswum," *Audience* (Advanced Edition) I (1970): 10-11. (Revised, reprinted, and retitled "Could World War I Have Been a Mistake?" in *The Last Carousel*.)

"A Ticket on Skoronski," *Saturday Evening Post*, CCXXXIX (November 5, 1966): 48-56. (Revised and reprinted in *The Last Carousel*.)

"The Unacknowledged Champion of Everything," *The Noble Savage*, 2 (September, 1960): 14-24.

3. Poetry

"The Bride Below the Black Coiffure," *Rogue*, IV, 7 (July, 1961): 30-31.

"Epitaph: *The Man with the Golden Arm*," *Poetry: A Magazine of Verse*, LXX (September, 1947): 316-17. (Reprinted in *The Last Carousel*.)

"Home and Goodnight," *Poetry: A Magazine of Verse*, LV (November, 1939): 74-76.

"How Long Blues," *Poetry: A Magazine of Verse*, LVIII (September, 1941): 309.

"Local South," *Poetry: A Magazine of Verse*, LVIII (September, 1941): 308-09. (Reprinted in *Encore*, I [February, 1942]: 75.)

"Nobody Knows," *Saturday Review*, XLIX (September 3, 1966): 15.

"Ode to an Absconding Bookie," *Chicago Sunday Tribune*, October 9, 1972. (Reprinted in *The Last Carousel*.)

"Sentiment with Terror," *Poetry: A Magazine of Verse*, LV (December, 1939): 157-59.

"Swede Was a Hard Guy," *Southern Review*, VII, 4 (1942): 873-79.

"Travelog," *Poetry: A Magazine of Verse*, LV (November, 1939): 76-77.

"Tricks Out of Times Long Gone," *Nation*, CXCV (September 22, 1962): 162. (Reprinted in *The Last Carousel*.)

4. Other Works: Articles, Sketches, Letters, Columns, Interviews, Discussions

"Airy Persiflage on the Heaving Deep *or* Sam, You Made the Ship too Short," *Works in Progress*, 1. (Reprinted in *The Last Carousel*.)

"Algren Writes of Roses and Hits," *Chicago Sun Times*, October 3, 1959.

"American Christmas, 1952," *Nation*, CLXXV (December 27, 1952): Inside Cover, 588.

"Blanche Sweet Under the Tapioca," *Chicago Sunday Tribune*, April 30, 1972. (Reprinted and retitled "Previous Days" in *The Last Carousel*.)

"Chicago Author Looks at French Culture and Finds It To Be Mostly American," *Chicago Sun Times*, June 26, 1949, 8x.

"Chicago is a Wose," *Nation*, CLXXXVII (February 28, 1959): 191.

"Do It the Hard Way," *The Writer*, LVI (March, 1943): 67-70.

"Eggheads Are Rolling: The Rush to Conform," *Nation*, CLXXVII (October 17, 1953): 306-07.

"Eight 'Angry Ones' Declare a British Existentialism," *Chicago Sun Times*, April 13, 1958.

"The Emblems and the Proofs of Power," *The Critic*, XXV, 4 (February, March, 1967): Front Cover and 20-25. (Reprinted in *Vagabond*, V [Summer, 1967]: 57-66.)

"Erik Dorn: A Thousand and One Afternoons in Nada" (Introduction to *Erik Dorn* by Ben Hecht.). Chicago: University of Chicago Press, pp. vii-xvii.

"Federal Art Projects: WPA: Literature," *The Chicago Artist*, I (December-January, 1937-1938): 6, 10.

"Fellini's 'La Dolce Vita': A Discussion by Nelson Algren, Mario De Vecchi, and Studs Terkel," *wmft Chicago Fine Arts Guide*, X, no. 8 (August, 1961): 5-9.

"For the Homeless Youth of America" (caption reads, "from his novel, *Native Son*), *Masses*, (March-April, 1934), p. 4.

"Hemingway: The Dye that Did Not Run," *Nation*, CXCIII (November 18, 1961): 387-90.

"Hollywood Djinn with a Dash of Bitters," *Nation*, CLXXVII (July 25, 1953): 68-70.

"The Hustlers" (excerpt from *Chicago: City on the Make*). *Art of the Essay*. Edited by L. H. Fiedler. New York: Thomas Y. Crowell Co., 1958. pp. 145-48.

"I Know They'll Like Me in Cholon," *The Critic*, XXVII, 4 (February-March, 1969): 58-61. (Revised, reprinted, and retitled "I Know They'll Like Me in Saigon" in *The Last Carousel*.)

Introduction to *The True Story of Bonnie and Clyde*. New York: The New American Library, Inc., 1968. (Reprinted and retitled "After the Buffalo" in *The Last Carousel*.)

"Letter from Saigon," *The Critic*, XXVIII (September-October, 1969): 14, 94. (A section is reprinted in *The Last Carousel*.)

"Letter to David Laing," *Inscape* (Winter-Spring, 1966): 63-64.

"The Mafia of the Heart," *Contact*, VI (September, 1960): 9-15.

"Merry Christmas, Mr. Mark!," *Chicago Sunday Tribune*, December 4, 1949. (Reprinted in *The Last Carousel*.)

"Nelson Algren Writes Impressions of Series," *Chicago Sun Times*, October 2, 1959. p. 5.

"Nelson Algren's Reflections: Hep-Ghosts of the Rain," *Chicago Sun Times*, October 10, 1959.

"No Cumshaw No Rickshaw," Part I, *Holiday*, XLIX (July, 1971): 32-35, 79.

"No Cumshaw No Rickshaw," Part II, *Holiday*, L (November, 1971): 44-47, 77, 80.

"One Man's Chicago," *Holiday*, X (October, 1951): 72-73, 75, 78, 80-83, 87-89, 117, 119.

"Otto Preminger's Strange Suspenjers," *Focus/Media*. Edited by Jess Ritter and Grover Lewis. New York: Chandler Publishing Company, 1972, pp. 10-18. (Revised and reprinted in *The Last Carousel*.)

"The Poet's Chicago" (excerpt from *Chicago: City on the Make*), *The Kiwanis Magazine* (March, 1958): 24-25.

"Remembering Richard Wright," *Nation*, CXCII (January 28, 1961): 85.

"Role of the Writer in America" (Literary Symposium sponsored by *Esquire Magazine* at the University of Michigan with Vance Bourjaily, William Styron, Nelson Algren, and Gore Vidal), *Michigan's Literary Quarterly: Voices*, II, 3 (Spring, 1962): 3-27.

"Some of the Authors of 1951, Speaking for Themselves," *New York Herald Tribune Book Review*, October 7, 1951, p. 27.

"Speaking Out: Down with the Cops" (Algren disclaims credit for this title), *Saturday Evening Post*, CCXXXVIII (October 23, 1965): 10-11.

"That Was No Albatross," *The Critic*, XXVII (April-May, 1969): 58-59, 96. (Sections reprinted and retitled "Letter from Saigon" in *The Last Carousel*.)

"They Don't Want To Belong to Us: Itinerant Journalist Goes Bamboo," *The Critic*, XXVIII (November-December, 1969): 76-81. (Reprinted and retitled "The Poor Girls of Kowloon" in *The Last Carousel*.)

"They're Hiding the Ham on the Pinball King, or Some Came Stumbling" (excerpt from *Who Lost an American?*), *Contact*, IX (September, 1961): 101-11.

"Things of the Earth: A Groundhog View" (excerpt from address delivered to writers' conferences and at Indiana University and the University of Missouri), *The California Quarterly*, II, 1 (Autumn, 1952): 3-11. Reprinted in *Pacific Citizen*, December 19, 1952, pp. 34-35.

"3 Tapes" (Interviews with Nelson Algren, Erskine Caldwell, and Meyer Levin), *Writer's Yearbook*, XXXI (1960): 45-49, 148, 150.

"The Way to Médenine," *Playboy*, XIX, 12 (December, 1972): 153, 222, 234, 239-40. (Reprinted and retitled "Brave Bulls of Sidi Yahya" in *The Last Carousel*.)

"White Mice and Mama-sans Get It all," *Rolling Stone*, May 27, 1971. (Reprinted and retitled "Police and Mama-sans Get It All" in *The Last Carousel.*)

"The Word Game: The Best Novels of World War II," *The Critic*, XXXI, 3 (January-February 1973): 74-77.

SECONDARY SOURCES

To date, with the exception of the Donohue interviews, no full-length studies of Algren have been published. Some of the following listings are excerpts from books; others have appeared in periodicals. No reviews of individual works are included here. Bibliographical information on reviews quoted in the text is provided in the Notes.

ALLSOP, K. (ed.) "A Talk on the Wild Side," *Spectator*, CCIII (October 16, 1959): 509-10. Interview in which Algren gives a brief summary of his life and career, concluding with his disillusionment with the "writing racket."

ANDERSON, ALSTON and TERRY SOUTHERN. "Nelson Algren," *Paris Review*, XI (Winter, 1955): 37-58. Reprinted in *Writers at Work: The Paris Review Interviews*. New York: The Viking Press, 1958. Algren's views on other writers, critics, his own work. One of the first interviews and still one of the best.

BLUESTONE, GEORGE. "Nelson Algren," *Western Review*, XXII (Autumn, 1957): 27-44. In perhaps the most perceptive criticism yet published, Bluestone, who contends that Algren is not a Naturalist and is only secondarily an urban writer, discusses the importance of the love and death themes in his fiction and the poetry and wit with which they are presented. Algren says that Bluestone "cuts in close" to the truth about his work.

BREIT, HARVEY. "The Writer Observed," *New York Times Book Review* (October 2, 1949), p. 33. (Also called "Talk with Nelson Algren" in this same issue. Reprinted as "Nelson Algren" in *The Writer Observed*. Cleveland: World Publishing Company, 1956. Account of a brief interview with Algren; concerned chiefly with his opinions about other writers.

CORRINGTON, JOHN WILLIAM. "Nelson Algren Talks with NOR's Editor-at-Large," *The New Orleans Review*, I, no. 2 (Winter, 1969): 130-32. The latest published interview which Corrington introduces by calling Algren one of the few "American" writers today, a "shaper of contemporary American literature." Algren answers questions about his first and last novels, Norman Mailer, Richard Daly, the New Left, his interest in other books, and the responsibility of the artist.

DE BEAUVOIR, SIMONE. "An American Rendezvous: The Question of Fidelity," Part II (translated by Richard Howard), *Harper's* CCXXIX (December, 1964): 111-22. An excerpt adapted from Miss de Beauvoir's autobiography, *The Force of Circumstance;* this is her latest resumé of her relationship with Algren about which she had written in *America Day by Day* and which she fictionized in *The Mandarins*.

DONOHUE, H. E. F. (with Nelson Algren). *Conversations with Nelson Algren*. New York: Hill and Wang, 1964. Transcriptions of taped conversations held in 1962 and 1963 concern Algren's ancestry, childhood, youth, Depression wanderings, army days, and his writing. Though unstructured, the conversations could, as Donohue suggests, be subtitled *Notes toward a Biography*.

EISINGER, CHESTER E. "Nelson Algren: Naturalism as the Beat of the Iron Heart," *Fiction of the Forties*. Chicago: University of Chicago Press, 1963, pp. 73-85. Discusses Algren as a Naturalist who writes with compassion and sensibility.

GEISMAR, MAXWELL. "Nelson Algren: The Iron Sanctuary," *College English*, XIV (March, 1953): 311-15. Reprinted in *English Journal*, XLII (March, 1963): 121-25 and in *American Moderns: From Rebellion to Conformity*. New York: Hill and Wang, 1958. Re-examination of Algren's work in which Geismar concludes that it represents an extreme phase of native American Realism: a world where human beings caught in the trap of social circumstance find prison, "an iron sanctuary," the safest place to be. Algren says "My Freudian friend, Max Geismar, cut in pretty close with his revelation of an iron sanctuary."

GELFANT, BLANCHE. *The American City Novel*. (Second Edition). Norman: The University of Oklahoma Press, 1970, pp. 252-57. Discusses Algren as an ecological novelist; his protagonist is a spacial unit wherein man searches for a complete self in an urban world whose inhabitants are bound together by a common background of disorder.

GLEASON, RALPH J. "Perspectives: Is It Out of Control?" *Rolling Stone* (August 6, 1970), p. 9. A brief article crediting Algren, especially in *A Walk on the Wild Side*, with the "fantasy/reality, inside/outside paradoxical view of the American Dream" which has influenced Heller, Kesey, and Bob Dylan.

LIPTON, LAWRENCE. "A Voyeur's View of the Wild Side: Nelson Algren and His Reviewers," *Chicago Review Anthology* (Winter, 1957), pp. 31-41. More than a summation of the reviews of reviewers of *A Walk on the Wild Side*, Lipton's article is a defense of Algren's words and ideas and a derisive reply to his critics, particularly to Fiedler, Podhoretz, and Gleason.

OMICK, ROBERT. "Compassion in the Novels of Nelson Algren." Unpublished doctoral dissertation, The University of Iowa, 1967. An examination of the structure, characters, imagery, and themes of Algren's fiction in an attempt to prove that he has made significant literature because of and out of true compassion.

RAY, DAVID, ed. "Talk on the Wild Side: A Bowl of Coffee with Nelson Algren," *The Reporter*, XX (June 11, 1959): 31-33. Brief description of

Chicago's Northwest side precedes the interview with Algren, in which he discusses, among other things, his meeting with Hemingway, his novels, Beatniks, footnote furies, *Time*, and J. C. Kornpoën, who had the greatest imagination of our day but who wrote nothing down.

Index